STUDIES IN THE
Competition policy

Paul Bennett and Martin Cave

Brunel,
The University of West London

Series Editor
Bryan Hurl
Head of Economics, Harrow School

HEINEMANN
EDUCATIONAL

Heinemann Educational Books Ltd
Halley Court, Jordan Hill, Oxford OX2 8EJ

OXFORD LONDON EDINBURGH
MADRID ATHENS BOLOGNA PARIS
MELBOURNE SYDNEY AUCKLAND SINGAPORE TOKYO
IBADAN NAIROBI HARARE GABORONE
PORTSMOUTH NH (USA)

© Paul Bennett and Martin Cave 1991

First published 1991

British Library Cataloguing in Publication Data
Bennett, Paul
Competition policy. – (Studies in the UK economy)
1. Great Britain. Competition
I. Title II. Cave, Martin III Series
338.60480941

ISBN 0 435 33013 6

Typeset and illustrated by Gecko Limited, Bicester, Oxon

Printed and bound in Great Britain by Clays Ltd, St Ives plc

Acknowledgements

The Publishers would like to thank the following for permission to reproduce copyright material:

Associated Examining Board for the questions on pp. 15 – 16 and 63; The Economist for the cartoons on pp. 18, 22 and 42; The Financial Times for Figure 5 on pp. 20 – 21, and the articles on pp. 41 – 42, 49, 64, 70 – 71 and 78; Reproduced with the permission of the Controller of Her Majesty's Stationery Office: the figures on p. 24 from the Monopolies and Mergers Commission, and Figure 6 on p. 26, Figure 7 on p. 29 and Figure 8 on p. 30 from the Department of Trade and Industry; The Independent on Sunday for the articles on pp. 44 and 58; Joint Matriculation Board for the question on p. 88; Oxford and Cambridge Schools Examination Board for the questions on pp. 34, 63 and 88; Southern Universities Joint Board for the questions on pp. 63 and 88; The Times for the articles on pp. 35, and 46 – 47; Tribune Media Services for the cartoon by Macnelly on p. 13 which appeared in the Chicago Tribune; University of Cambridge Delegacy of Local Examinations for the question on p. 88; University of London School Examinations Board for the questions on pp. 15, 16, 34, 77 and 78; University of Oxford Local Examinations Syndicate for the questions on pp. 16, 34, 48 and 63; Welsh Joint Education Committee for the questions on pp. 34 and 48.

The publishers have made every effort to contact the correct copyright holders. However, if any material has been incorrectly acknowledged, the publishers would be pleased to make the necessary arrangements at the earliest opportunity

The authors wish to acknowledge the valuable assistance of Yogesh Sharma and Lior Jussur, and to thank David Higham for his helpful comments on the manuscript. We retain, however, full responsibility for the final text. Our grateful thanks are also due to Sally Harris for her highly efficient typing and amendment of the manuscript.

Contents

Preface   *iv*

Chapter One   Introduction   1

Chapter Two   The basic economics of monopolies,
                  mergers and restrictive practices   4

Chapter Three   UK competition policy in practice   17

Chapter Four   Monopoly policy   36

Chapter Five   Mergers policy in the UK   50

Chapter Six   Anti-competitive practices   65

Chapter Seven   Regulating monopoly utilities   79

Index   90

Preface

Some parts of an Economics syllabus seem to be intrinsically more interesting than others. The strength of *competition policy* as a concept is that, after abstractions on the theory of the firm, the clouds roll away and real, household-name firms materialize, understanding quickens and pupils find that what is dealt with in class also features in the Press and on television.

Many teachers have cause to be grateful to the authors for their contributions to the annual Brunel Economics Update Course and will not need convincing that this book continues that standard. For those who do need convincing, consider what is written in the introductory chapter:

> *'Competition issues are not only among the most challenging but also among the most exciting in economics.'*

The cautious or the sceptical might consider this a soft sell: the committed know this to be no idle hyperbole.

This volume is a model of clear exposition from two enthusiasts. It contains an up-to-date account of the theory and practice of competition policy in the United Kingdom. It outlines the general principles involved, sets out and evaluates existing UK and European Commission regulations, and examines policy and performance in four major areas – the treatment of monopolistic firms; mergers policy; anti-competitive practices which restrict or distort competition; and regulated, recently privatized, industries such as gas or electricity which, by their very nature, are likely to be monopolistic.

Bryan Hurl
Series Editor

Chapter One
Introduction

. . . governments are constantly facing up to dilemmas in their management of competition where it is difficult to decide whether a particular course of action which a firm wants to undertake will in the long term restrict or enhance competition.

This book is about the policy which governments can and should adopt towards maintaining competition within the economy. Ever since the time of Adam Smith and before, economists have regarded competition as playing an important and – most people believe – a beneficial role in the economy. The existence of competitors, or even the threat of them, makes firms strive to produce the best product they can at the lowest price in order to retain or expand their market share. In most economic analysis, competitive pressures of this kind are seen as providing a vital stimulus towards efficiency and innovation. Monopoly, which is the extreme case of the absence of competition, is seen by contrast as creating an environment in which firms can get away with providing a low quality of product or of service, charging high prices, and pursuing their own interests rather than those of their customers.

If this were all there is to the economic analysis of competition, then competition policy would be very straightforward. The government would simply seek to ensure that all industries contained a sufficient number of competitors; when it found monopolies, the government would break them up. Unfortunately, however, the argument is not so simple. In the first place, there may be advantages in terms of cost savings in having all customers for a product supplied by a single firm. If production in an industry benefits from economies of scale, then a monopoly may in principle be the most efficient way of meeting demand. In a situation of this kind, a balance has to be struck between the advantages of competition and the advantages of size.

More generally, governments are constantly facing up to dilemmas in their management of competition where it is difficult to decide whether a particular course of action which a firm wants to undertake will in the long term restrict or enhance competition. Consider the following examples:

(1) In 1989, the government allowed GEC and Siemens, two large German electrical firms, jointly to take over Plessey, a smaller British company in the electrical and telecommunications industry. The argument against the takeover was that it would reduce competition in the UK in the electrical goods sector. The argument in favour of it was that it would create larger and stronger European firms in the industry which could compete more effectively with the giant firms of the USA and Japan. Does the takeover enhance or restrict competition?

(2) One of the major changes in transport policy over the last five years has been the opening up of the bus industry to increased competition. When a new firm comes in to provide a competing service on a bus route, the original firm often cuts its prices. Is this a natural and beneficial consequence of competition, or is it an attempt by the original firm to drive the entrant out of business and re-establish its monopoly?

(3) Several professions (lawyers, doctors, etc.) have until recently restricted their members' capacity to advertise for clients. Is this an attempt to prevent the public 'shopping around' to find the best value for money, or is it a perfectly reasonable restriction which prevents the public being exploited by incompetent, cost-cutting practitioners?

(4) The telephone system in the UK is dominated by British Telecom, which has about 95 per cent of the market (the remaining 5 per cent belonging to Mercury plc). The government has nurtured Mercury as a competitor for BT, but now faces the dilemma of whether to allow additional competitors in the market. If a third firm comes in, it might damage Mercury, and strengthen rather than weaken BT's virtual monopoly. Should further entry be permitted?

All these examples, which are considered in more detail in the chapters which follow, illustrate the very difficult practical problems of analysis and judgement which arise in debates about competition policy.

Competition issues are not only among the most challenging but also among the most exciting in economics. Major takeover battles provide one of the most dramatic forms of theatre in the business world. They are fought out in the full glare of publicity by company executives and their financial and legal advisers. Often tens of millions of pounds (or in the USA, hundreds of millions of dollars) are at stake for the individual participants. For example, the contested takeover of RJR Nabisco for $25 billion, netted gigantic sums for the principals involved and left both winners and losers with bills from advisers to the value of hundreds of millions of dollars. Sums nearly as large were at stake in the attempt made by three prominent financiers to take over BAT plc, a major UK company. Even more dramatically, the takeover of Distillers by Guinness plc led to the conviction and imprisonment of the Guinness Chairman and several of his financial associates for serious criminal offences. Successful, and sometimes even unsuccessful, takeover bids can have equally significant if less publicized consequences for the workforces of the companies involved. They may lead to closures and rationalizations in which tens of thousands of workers lose their jobs.

In this book we set out the basic economic principles underlying competition policy and illustrate these principles by some major case studies, of monopolies, mergers and anti-competitive practices. The organization of the book is as follows. Chapter 2 sets out an approach to evaluating the costs and benefits of competition or monopoly. Chapter 3 explains the framework of law within which British companies operate – both UK law and law of the European Community. Chapter 4 analyses in more detail, with case studies, instances where a single firm controls a large proportion of the market and considers the appropriate policy responses. Chapter 5 deals with the often controversial issue of whether mergers or takeovers should be permitted. Chapter 6 looks at ways in which firms can behave either singly or in concert in a way which is anti-competitive. Finally, Chapter 7 examines those special industries, including electricity, gas, telecommunications and water, where the government has taken special powers to regulate the dominant suppliers more directly than through normal competition law.

Reading list

Livesey, F., Chapter 10 in *Textbook of Economics*, 3rd edn, Longman, 1989.

Chapter Two

The basic economics of monopolies, mergers and restrictive practices

... monopolization may cause harm to the economy by raising prices, but in some industries there may be compensating efficiency from having larger firms.

This chapter gives a brief account of the basic economic analysis of competition and monopoly, which is needed to understand competition policy. Much of it will already be familiar from standard textbooks, and those seeking a fuller account may want to consult the reading list at the end of this chapter to guide them to it. It is, however, essential to have a clear grasp of the analysis of competitive and monopolistic markets which underlies policy on monopolies and mergers. It is also useful to be acquainted with the terminology which is often used in accounts of takeovers and related episodes in the financial Press. A guide to this terminology is given towards the end of the chapter.

Competition and monopoly

Perfect competition and monopoly represent the extreme cases of market structure. Under perfect competition, there are so many firms and each firm is so small in relation to the market as a whole that its impact on prices is negligible. In other words, the perfectly competi-

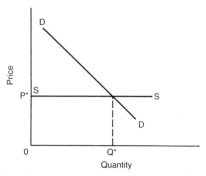

Figure 1 The competitive industry

tive firm is a price-taker: it has to maximize its profits taking as given the price of output determined in the market as a whole. The long-run equilibrium of a perfectly competitive industry is shown in Figure 1. The equilibrium position occurs at the point where the supply curve SS (which reflects marginal costs) crosses the demand curve DD, at output level Q*. (For simplicity we have assumed a horizontal long-run supply curve. In other words, if demand expands, new firms come into the industry producing at the same level of costs as existing ones. But the argument goes through just as well with an upward-sloping supply curve.) At the long-run equilibrium, each firm is maximizing its profits at the going price P*, and the right number of firms are in the industry to ensure that each firm is making normal but not excessive profits.

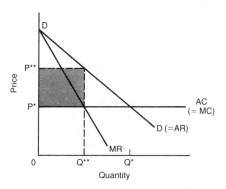

Figure 2 Price and quantity chosen by a monopolist

We can contrast the case of a perfectly competitive industry with that of a monopolist, the situation observed at the other end of the spectrum of possible market structures. The equilibrium position of a monopolist is illustrated in Figure 2. In a monopoly, only one firm supplies the market and the demand curve for the firm (DD) is thus the demand curve for the market: it is therefore downward-sloping. The monopolist's marginal revenue (MR) lies beneath the demand or average revenue curve, reflecting the fact that, in order to sell an extra unit of output, the monopolist must lower the price from that of previous units sold. The firm's average cost (AC) and marginal cost (MC) levels are assumed equal for simplicity. The firm maximizes profits where MC and MR are equal – otherwise an increase or a decrease in output would make the firm more money. (For example, at a point to the right of Q**, MC exceeds MR, indicating that the firm is making a net loss on the last unit of

5

output produced. This should be a signal to cut output back. Conversely, to the left of Q**, MR exceeds MC so that the firm is foregoing a profit opportunity by cutting back output.) The price the monopolist will charge is P**. The monopolist's excess profit, therefore, is represented by the shaded area in Figure 2: it is selling Q** units and making a profit of P** minus AC on each of them.

This is the **super-normal** (or excess) **profit** made in addition to the 'normal' profit made by a competitive firm and needed to pay the dividends etc. which shareholders require to continue investing in any firm. If firms in an industry are making below normal profits, some of them will leave. If super-normal profits are being made, others will be attracted in unless there are entry barriers of the kind discussed in Chapter 4.

We thus have two extreme results. Under perfect competition, each firm just breaks even, while the monopolist illustrated in Figure 2 is able to raise the price above average and marginal cost and thus make an excess profit.

It is important to be clear about the nature of the harm done to the economy by monopolies. One objection to monopoly profits is that they represent a form of **exploitation** of the consumer and generate an unequal distribution of income. Owners of, or shareholders in, monopoly firms enjoy their extra profits at the expense of ordinary households. Provided we are willing to make the appropriate value judgement about income distribution (and provided monopoly *does* benefit the rich at the expense of the poor) this is a powerful argument against it.

A more subtle argument against monopoly is that it introduces an overall distortion into the operation of the economy and leads to avoidable **welfare losses.** This argument is illustrated in Figure 3. If the output level in the industry is Q* (the 'competitive' case), the costs of production are represented by area OP*CQ*, as average costs are constant at level OP*. The valuation which households collectively place upon output Q* is represented by the area under the demand curve (AD) up to output level Q*. Thus we see that households are willing to pay a sum in excess of the average cost of production for the first unit of the product which they consume, while for the final unit at Q* they are only prepared to pay the average cost of production. That excess of consumers' willingness to pay over what they are required to pay is called **consumers' surplus** and is represented in Figure 3 by the triangle P*AC.

Now imagine that the industry is monopolized and output falls to Q** while price rises to P**. Consumer surplus has now shrunk to

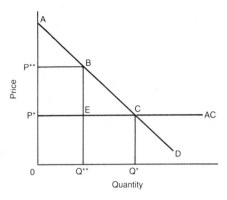

Figure 3 The monopoly welfare loss

area ABP**. Of the consumer surplus lost, a proportion, represented by the rectangle P*P**BE, is converted into profits for the monopolist. This amount is thus not lost but transferred from consumers' surplus to monopoly profits. But the smaller triangle BCE is irretrievably lost as the result of the monopolization of production.

The intuition behind this geometric argument is as follows. Ideally, we want to present consumers with prices which reflect marginal costs so that when they are allocating their budget between different products they make decisions on the basis of relative prices which reflect the costs to the economy of producing the goods in question. Under perfect competition, this condition is satisfied because price and marginal cost are equal. But a monopoly puts a wedge between price (P**) and marginal cost (P*) and distorts consumers' purchases. The cost of this distortion is shown in Figure 3 by triangle BCE.

Several economists have tried to estimate the size of the loss from monopoly in the UK economy by measuring the extent to which monopoly prices exceed competitive ones in the various sectors (the gap between P** and P* in Figure 3) and the resulting decline in output from the competitive case (distance Q**Q* in the figure). Although there is dispute about the size of the effect, estimates of monopoly welfare loss amount to 4–7 per cent of the gross national product.

This is a precise way of trying to quantify the potential harm done to the economy by monopolies, and one which we shall find very useful in our discussion of the desirability of mergers. It was formulated above in terms of the contrast between the extreme cases of perfect competition and monopoly, but it can also be applied more generally. In practice observed market structures are likely to fall somewhere in between the two extremes. The more relevant comparison thus lies between industries which exhibit 'workable' competition – i.e. a sufficient degree of rivalry between firms to ensure that prices are forced down to something approximating marginal cost – and those which may have more than one firm but which nonetheless have prices above marginal costs because those firms have established a relationship which eliminates much price competition. Fortunately, the analysis above is sufficiently general to take in these more realistic cases. Figure 1 can be extended to include cases of workable competition where price and marginal cost are roughly but not exactly the same, and Figure 2 can be adapted to accommodate industries which have a small number of firms earning high profits but which are not pure monopolies.

In trying to establish which firms exercise monopoly power, it is not enough simply to count the number of firms in an industry. Market power also depends upon the ease with which potential entrants can come into the industry if high profits are being made. Markets subject to potential entry of this kind are known as **contestable** and the threat of competition in them should be enough to keep prices down. In practice, however, most industries are not subject to this discipline, as potential entrants are deterred by the prospect of heavy losses if firms already in the industry lower their prices. But the contestability argument does show that there is no necessary link between a small number of firms and the degree of monopoly power exercised.

The final important step towards realism taken here is to recognize that competition within industries takes place over time. Most industries do not produce a single homogeneous product, and firms compete in terms of quality and innovation as well as in terms of price. At any time, a firm may have a temporary monopoly of a particular product as a result of its own efforts in design and innovation. But this is not likely to be a serious cause for concern if that temporary monopoly is continuously threatened by other firms.

Analysis of mergers

The framework set out above is particularly suited to the analysis of mergers. So far, monopolization seems to bring only costs and no benefits. But the claim is often made that two firms, by joining together, will be able to rationalize their production and achieve economies of scale; that is, to lower unit costs of production. This benefit should be weighed in the balance against the costs of greater concentration.

A way of doing so is illustrated in Figure 4. An industry initially consisted of many firms, producing at an average cost of AC_1 with the price of output at average cost (OP*). The firms then merged to form a monopoly, and the new monopoly firm raised the price of output to OP**, while output fell to Q**. By our former analysis, the resulting monopoly welfare loss is represented by triangle BCE. Suppose, however, that the new firm is able to lower its costs to the level AC_2. This will generate an efficiency gain equal to rectangle P'P*EF (the shaded area). This efficiency gain may exceed, equal, or be less than the welfare loss triangle BCE.

This approach suggests a possible **cost–benefit calculation** to demonstrate whether a merger should be allowed to proceed. The investigation requires estimates both of the extent to which the merged firm will be able to raise prices (and thus cause a welfare loss) and of the cost savings which may result from the merger. Under this procedure, the government or the competition authority would have to estimate the relative areas and decide whether the gains from the merger would be likely to outweigh the losses. An example is given in the boxed exhibit.

This approach to evaluating merger proposals has been influential in the United Kingdom and some particular examples of attempts to quantify costs and benefits are given in Chapter 5. Many firms seeking to merge with or take over companies often hold out the prospect of substantial efficiency gains.

Fortunately, we are now in a position to evaluate these claims over a substantial sample of mergers. The method used is to compare the profitability of the merged firm with the profitability of the constituent firms before the merger. If efficiency gains are occurring, profit rates should go up. If profit rates *do not* go up, this suggests that the efficiency gains are illusory. The comparison required is in practice rather more difficult than this, as some allowance has to be made for changing levels of profitability in the economy overall. But when such allowance is made, the weight of evidence suggests that mergers do *not* increase profitability. This is a surprising and perhaps rather disconcerting result, which does, however, require further investigation for it to be accepted as conclusive.

If this argument suggests that mergers are not always justified on efficiency grounds, there is another argument which operates in favour of at least allowing the possibility of takeovers. This second argument suggests that the threat of takeover may have an impor-

Competition policy

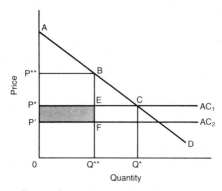

Figure 4 Welfare effects of a merger

The efficiency of a merger

This numerical example illustrates the cost–benefit approach to merger appraisal. Initially, output in the competitive industry is 30 units per year, sold at their cost of £6 per unit (see the figure). When the companies merge, output falls to 20 per year and the price rises to £10. The resulting loss of consumer surplus is shown by the shaded triangle, whose area is:

$1/2 \times (30 - 20) \times (10 - 6) = 20$

Now suppose the merger also lowers average costs to £4 per unit. That cost saving is shown in the shaded rectangle; its area is:

$(6 - 4) \times 20 = 40$

We thus find a cost saving of £40 per year and a loss of consumer surplus of £20. The merger should go ahead. If only real merger inquiries were as simple as this example!

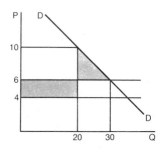

tant influence on a firm's management. If a firm is free from the risk of takeover, its management can be slack and inefficient. The executives may spend many working hours on the golf course and spend extravagantly on perks. (The story is told that a well-known American takeover specialist regularly flies first class on US domestic airlines and falls into conversation with fellow passengers. When he discovers that a company's executives are enjoying this expensive perk, he considers it as a possible takeover target – arguing that the management is inefficient and the true potential of the assets is not being realized.) When, however, firms are constantly under the

TAKEOVER OF THE IMPERIAL GROUP BY HANSON TRUST

Hanson Trust is now one of the largest companies in the UK after a series of substantial takeovers in the 1980s. One of Hanson's major successes was the takeover in 1986 of the Imperial Group. This took place after an announcement by the Imperial Group and United Biscuits of an agreed merger provoked Hanson Trust to make an offer for the Imperial Group, valuing it at £1.8 billion. The offer was strongly rejected by the Imperial management.

In early 1986, a classic takeover battle for Imperial developed between Hanson and United Biscuits. Hanson finally received acceptances of more than 50 per cent of Imperial's shares, and took the company over.

Following the change in ownership, the chairman and chief executive of Imperial resigned, accompanied by five non-executive directors and three executive directors. In the following two years Hanson sold off the bulk of Imperial assets and was able to make substantial pre-tax profits on those which it retained.

The UK and the USA are in the minority of countries permitting a relatively free market in takeovers. In most of continental Europe and Japan, various regulations would have frustrated the restructuring of Imperial by a hostile acquiring company and the wholesale change in its management. The example thus illustrates how the market for corporate control operates fairly freely in the UK.

threat of takeover, the management will be forced by market pressures to behave efficiently. This argument suggests that the stock market in which shares of a target company can be bought is 'a **market for corporate control**'. Evidence of the effectiveness of this 'market' is inconclusive, but the observation that mergers do not increase profitability does not show that it is ineffective: perhaps most opportunities for profitable takeovers are already exploited.

In the UK the market for corporate control is fairly unrestricted, whereas in the rest of Europe – notably France and Germany – there are many restrictions on the ability of the acquiring firm to alter employment of both workers and managers in the target firm if the takeover succeeds. In the UK, by contrast, it is normal for the directors of an acquired company to resign (or be dismissed) and for substantial restructuring to occur. This is illustrated in the Hanson Trust/Imperial Group example on page 11.

Collusion and restrictive practices

Competition within an industry can be undermined not only by a single firm becoming dominant through internal growth or takeover, but also through **collusion** among the firms in the industry. Thus firms might agree not to undercut one another in bidding for contracts; or they might agree to maintain a common price and limit their competition to non-price elements, such as quality and design.

It is hard to see how such arrangements could benefit consumers, except in rather special circumstances. A collusive arrangement of this kind raises prices for consumers without offering any potential efficiency gains. The latter are not available because the individual firms continue to produce separately, and no rationalization of production occurs of the kind made possible by mergers. It is therefore not surprising that, as shown in Chapter 3, the law on collusive arrangements of this kind is tougher than it is on mergers.

The language of takeovers

Over the past ten years, a specialized language has arisen to describe what occurs during mergers and takeovers. It is useful to have some understanding of the processes involved and the terms used to describe them. Many of the terms originate in the USA, but they are also used in the British context.

When a firm wants to take over another firm, it will typically begin by acquiring a proportion of the target's *shares*. In both the USA and Europe – for reasons more to do with protecting investors than promoting competition – there are restrictions on the proportion of shares one firm can acquire in another without disclosing its holding or being required to make an offer for further shares.

These rules mean that typically an acquiring company will buy up to 10 per cent of the shares in the target without disclosure (perhaps in what is known as a **dawn raid** – a sudden entry on to the stock market), and will then disclose its holding and make an offer to buy further shares at a stipulated price. As soon as the disclosure has been made, the acquirer can extend its holding up to 30 per cent on the open market but must stop there. It is then up to all shareholders to vote on whether or not to accept the takeover offer. If a majority votes to accept, the acquirer must buy as many shares as sellers are willing to dispose of at the offer price. Acquiring companies need not offer cash to shareholders in the target company; they may choose to offer shares in their own company instead, or a combination of cash and shares.

The acquiring company may be a firm which is already trading, but in some cases it may be a company which is specially established to carry out the takeover. This is likely to be the case if the management of a firm wants to undertake a **management buyout** (MBO); that is, to buy it from its shareholders and run it themselves. In these circumstances, the managers will establish a company especially for the purpose, seek to borrow money from the banks or other financial institutions, and offer to buy shares from the shareholders. An alternative variant which became common in the USA in the

Cartoon by Macnelly reprinted from Chicago Tribune, by permission of Tribune Media Services

1980s is what is called a **leveraged buyout** (LBO). In an LBO, a number of investors will borrow large amounts of money at a fixed interest from financial institutions and use that money to make an offer for the target firm. As soon as the target firm has been acquired, the new owners will typically sell off bits of it and use the cash thus realized to pay off their debts to the financial institutions. Some gigantic LBOs have taken place in the USA, notably a contested bid of $25 billion for RJR Nabisco, the food and tobacco conglomerate (see the reading list: Burrough and Helyar), and a smaller number have occurred in Britain, notably of Gateway, the supermarket chain.

There are often considerable risks to those who lend to a company carrying out an LBO, and financial institutions lending in this way will require high rates of interest on the bonds which they buy from the LBO company; if the takeover goes wrong, the bonds may become worthless. High-interest bonds issued to finance risky takeovers are known in the financial world as **junk bonds**. A measure of the risk of such investments is given by the fact that the market value of junk bonds in many corporations has declined to 20 cents in the dollar or less.

A company threatened with an unwelcome takeover has a number of defences at its disposal, depending upon the regulations applying in the relevant country. For instance, the target may adopt **poison pill tactics**; that is, it may seek to make itself unattractive to the acquiring company. This may involve the target company selling off assets which it knows the acquiring company particularly desires, or the target company itself carrying out a merger or takeover which will render it less attractive to the acquirer – perhaps because the later takeover would be prohibited by the government on monopoly grounds. Alternatively, the target company may seek to merge or be taken over by a more palatable acquirer; this is known as looking for a **white knight**. In the USA the target company may itself buy the shares from the acquiring company. In these circumstances, the acquirer builds up a holding in the target, which it then sells at a profit to the target itself. This practice is known as **greenmail** and is not permitted in the UK, though practised in the USA.

Conclusions

This chapter has set out the basic economics underlying competition policy. We have seen that monopolization may cause harm to the economy by raising prices, but that in some industries there may be compensating efficiency gains from having larger firms. This suggests that there is a case for analysing monopolies or mergers on a case by case basis and seeking to establish advantages and disadvantages of any particular situation. In cases where firms collude with one another to raise prices, however, there is a presumption that the practice is detrimental to efficiency.

KEY WORDS

Super-normal profit	Dawn raid
Exploitation	Management buyout
Welfare losses	Leveraged buyout
Consumers' surplus	Junk bonds
Contestable	Poison pill tactics
Cost–benefit calculation	White knight
Market for corporate control	Greenmail
Collusion	

Reading list

Burningham, D. *et al.*, *Understanding Economics,* 3rd edn, chap. 7, Hodder & Stoughton, 1991.

Burrough, B. and Helyar, J., *Barbarians at the Gate,* Jonathan Cape, 1990.

Davies, G. and Davies, J., 'The revolution in monopoly theory', *Lloyds Bank Review,* July 1984.

James, S., 'Welfare triangles and economic policy analysis', *Economics: Journal of the Economics Association,* Summer 1989.

Maunder, P., Myers, D., Wall, N. and LeRoy Miller, R., Chapters 23 and 24 in *Economics Explained: A Coursebook in A-Level Economics,* Collins Educational, 1987.

McDonald, F.E., 'Contestable markets – a new ideal model?', *Economics,* Spring 1987.

Rees, R. and Baxter, R. E., 'The great diamond monopoly', in *Readings in Economics,* book 1, part 5, Collins Educational, 1984.

Essay topics

1. 'Monopoly is in the public interest because it is efficient to have firms producing on a large scale.' Discuss.
   [University of London School Examinations Board, 1986]
2. Why may firms wish to reduce competition by colluding with each other; for example, by forming a cartel? Is such a collusion

in the public interest and what might be the economic effects of prohibiting collusion?
[Associated Examining Board, 1990]
3. What losses to the community are supposed to result from the existence of monopoly?
[University of Oxford Local Examinations Syndicate, 1986]
4. Examine the main differences in the determination of price and output in conditions of monopoly and oligopoly.
[University of London School Examinations Board, 1988]

Chapter Three
UK competition policy in practice

There is a sound economic basis for the Europeanization of competition policy, even though this must be at the expense of some degree of national sovereignty.

In Chapter 2 we established the theoretical basis for government intervention and regulation. This chapter examines the way in which competition policy operates in the UK and the European Community (EC). The present system of regulation is outlined, and this is followed by an evaluation of the effectiveness of current policy, and a discussion of its strengths and weaknesses.

The framework of UK competition policy
Competition policy is concerned with four broad areas: monopoly, anti-competitive practices, mergers, and restrictive trade practices. In each of these areas, there are several regulatory bodies which may have an interest in the conduct of firms and the structure of markets. EC competition law governs those issues which affect trade between member states, whilst UK law relates to competition within the UK.

In recent years there have been substantial changes in the operation of competition policy. These include:

- a greatly increased role for the European Commission, including the introduction of new merger controls;
- simplification of the criteria for investigation of merger proposals (the 'Tebbit Rules');
- proposals to strengthen the enforcement of government rulings on competition policy, and to introduce substantial and predictable penalties for disobeying rulings.

Although proposals on the last point have yet to be enacted, the intention is to bring UK practice into line with EC competition rules on enforcement (outlined below).

There are five principal competition authorities. These are:

(1) the European Commission;
(2) the Department of Trade and Industry, headed by the Secretary of State for Trade;

(3) the Office of Fair Trading (OFT);
(4) the Monopolies and Mergers Commission (MMC);
(5) the Restrictive Trade Practices Court (RTPC).

The European Commission
The European Commission is the executive arm of the European Community. There are 17 commissioners, who are generally former politicians from member countries. Commissioners give an undertaking to renounce their national interests when considering community issues. Each Commissioner has responsibility for a particular policy area (e.g. agriculture, education, etc.). The current competition commissioner is Sir Leon Brittan, a former UK trade secretary. He presides over an office consisting mainly of civil servants from member countries, whose function is to examine and investigate competition issues.

European Community competition policy
Articles 85 and 86 of the Treaty of Rome lay out the main provisions of European competition law, which is applicable in the United Kingdom. Article 85 bans agreements and restrictive practices which have the effect of limiting or distorting competition within the Common Market and which affect trade between member states. Exemptions can be sought under Article 85(3) on grounds of efficiency and economic progress and some classes of agreement (such as franchising) are subject to block exemptions. Article 86 prohibits the abuse of a **dominant position** with the Common Market by a firm insofar as it affects trade between

Policing Europe's single market: the European Commision is taking on more duties member states. 'Dominant' is not defined precisely, unlike UK legislation, where a 25 per cent market share is specified.

The Commission in many ways has more extensive powers than any single agency in the UK. It can initiate investigations, it can respond to complaints from other companies or individuals, and undertake its own investigations. The Commission must consult an advisory committee of member states before taking a formal decision under Article 85 or 86. Its powers of enforcement are stronger than those under current UK legislation. The Commission can fine firms up to 10 per cent of their turnover if they are found to have operated anti-competitive agreements or abused a dominant position. Firms can appeal against the Commission's decisions to the European Court of Justice. The decisions of the European Court are final. The flow chart in Figure 5, which is based on the London Underground map, illustrates the process.

There is a sound economic basis for the Europeanization of competition policy, even though this must be at the expense of some degree of national sovereignty. As the European market becomes increasingly integrated, firms in all countries will tend to do a higher proportion of business across national borders, throughout the EC. Leaving competition issues to national regulators may be inadequate for several reasons.

- The most obvious reason is that the national regulator will have difficulty in controlling what firms do outside their home country. A British firm may compete in the domestic market, so that there is no cause for British regulators to interfere. But it may join an anti-competitive cartel in Spain with other foreign firms which the Spanish authorities have difficulty in controlling.
- National regulators may be tempted to turn a blind eye to anti-competitive practices if the result is a net overall gain to their own economy. If a British firm acts in a monopolistic way throughout the EC, all European consumers will in effect pay. Even if British consumers are also losing, the excess profits from the whole of Europe are being returned to the UK economy. Regulators in Britain may view the costs and benefits solely from the British viewpoint and stand back. Regulators for Europe as a whole would take into account the monopolistic costs for Europe as a whole, and act more toughly.
- National regulators of domestic industries run the risk of ending up as protectors rather than policemen. **Regulatory capture** may occur, where the government department acts as a lobby for the

Competition policy

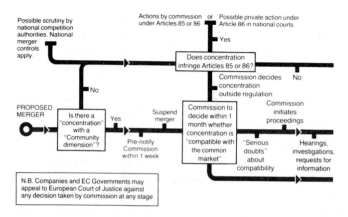

Figure 5 A flow chart for Euro-mergers. Source: *Financial Times*, 21 September 1990.

industry rather than protecting consumers. For example, national car manufacturers may end up by being protected from international competition by their industry ministeries, at the expense of consumers. This is less likely to occur where regulation is on a supra-national basis. (Though, to be sure, there is still the danger of a 'Fortress Europe' attitude to external competition, building trade barriers against the rest of the world.)

From September 1990, under the new EC's new **Merger Control Regulation**, the EC Commission took over responsibility for regulation of 'big' mergers, with national competition authorities accepting a reduced role, in effect ceding sovereignty in large-scale mergers.

The intention is to ensure a simplified regulatory structure in which there is no chance of overlap between the regulatory roles of the Commission and national authority. However, as Figure 5 shows, this objective has not been met in practice. The flow chart shows all the possible paths which a 'megamerger' could take before approval or rejection.

The chart exaggerates the complexity of the new system, since most 'megamergers' would proceed along the 'Central line' route from left to right of the chart, and proceedings will end at the four-month Commission decision point. Alternatively they will take the 'Northern line' for examination under Articles 85 and 86.

The idea is to eliminate the situation in which merger proposals could be reviewed by both the national regulators and the commission, and receive the green light from one, only to be stopped by the

UK competition policy in practice

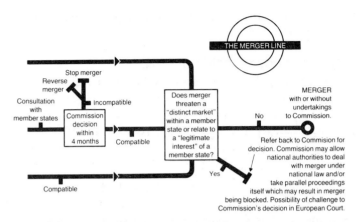

other. In principle, firms will in future not be faced with this 'double jeopardy'. Instead new merger regulations should provide **one-stop shopping**: a merger is referred *either* to the EC *or* to the national competition authorities, but not both.

In order to provide this, a series of clear tests has been devised. A merger will be considered by the EC (alone) if it:

(a) involves companies with a combined turnover of over 5 billion ECUs; *and*
(b) each company has a turnover within the EC of at least 250 million ECUs; *and*
(c) each company has no more than two-thirds of its EC turnover in the same country.

So, essentially, if a merger is (1) big, (2) within the EC, and (3) involves countries which trade outside their home market – then it will be dealt with by the European Commission alone.

However, it is still possible for the UK authorities to intervene and carry out their own investigation if the EC clears a 'megamerger':

(1) if national interests are at stake; *or*
(2) if competition in local markets is threatened.

If either of these clauses should be invoked by the UK authorities, then the one-stop shopping principle would be breached. Since both clauses *could* in principle be widely interpreted, that possibility certainly exists. The danger is that different national governments will attempt to second-guess the Commission if dissatisfied with its verdict, and conduct their own regulatory reviews all over again. Figure 5 shows the scope for mergers being side-tracked to national authorities for additional investigation. Similarly there may be problems if the Competition Commissioner takes a more political line than at present.

Competition policy within the UK

UK competition policy is governed by four principal acts of parliament. These are:

(1) the Competition Act 1980;
(2) the Restrictive Trade Practices Act 1976;
(3) the Resale Prices Act 1976;
(4) the Fair Trading Act 1973.

As already mentioned, the main **regulatory bodies** are the Secretary of State for Trade and Industry, the OFT, the MMC and the RTPC. In principle, and at the expense of some slight oversimplification, the roles of these agents are as follows.

The Secretary of State for Trade and Industry

The Secretary of State for Trade and Industry has overall responsibility for UK competition policy. He or she is a politician, a member of the Cabinet; and the job of Trade Secretary, as the incumbent is generally known, has proved to be something of a hot seat, with a rapid turnover of occupants in recent years, though competition policy issues have not always been responsible for this.

The role of the Trade Secretary is that of ultimate decision taker. In merger issues (but not investigations of existing monopolies), it is

the Trade Secretary who makes the decision on whether or not a merger should be referred to the MMC (advised by the **Director General of Fair Trading**). The Secretary also decides on the action to be taken in response to an MMC enquiry, and in effect approves or disapproves the OFT's work in obtaining undertakings from firms if necessary. Ultimately, if satisfactory undertakings cannot be reached, the Secretary has the power to make a legally binding order to implement his or her decisions. Ultimate powers of decision rest with the Secretary of State.

Office of Fair Trading

The OFT, headed by the Director General of Fair Trading (DGFT), is a government agency which plays a general supervisory role in competition policy, keeping markets under surveillance to ensure that firms comply with the various legislation. The OFT conducts its own preliminary investigations to establish whether action is required. The DGFT undertakes discussions with firms in order to achieve voluntary **compliance** with legislation in the case of monopolies, anti-competitive practices, and restrictive practices issues. In merger cases he can enter preliminary discussions with firms to establish whether the Trade Secretary will be advised to intervene, and whether firms can take action to avoid **reference** to the MMC – for example, by selling off subsidiaries which would gain a dominant market share. This is referred to as "divestment".

If voluntary agreement with firms cannot be reached, the DGFT can then refer the case directly to the MMC or the RTPC as appropriate, for a full investigation *except* in merger cases. In the case of mergers, the DGFT can only *advise* the Secretary of State whether or not to refer the case to the MMC. The Trade Secretary can accept or reject the DGFT's advice, and occasionally that advice is not taken, though this is unusual.

The DGFT is responsible for monitoring the compliance of any undertakings given by firms, in response to investigations, whether by the MMC, the RTP, or the OFT itself. Essentially the OFT plays several roles – investigator, consultant and adviser to the Secretary of State.

The Monopolies and Mergers Commission

The role of the MMC is to conduct investigations referred to it by the DGFT or the Trade Secretary, and to produce a report with recommendations. The Commission has a full-time chairman, appointed by the Trade Secretary, and consists of a 'panel' of salaried part-time members, drawn from business, the professions, trade unions and academics. There are currently 30 members on the panel, though with recent increases in the Commission's workload (see Table 1) the ceiling has been raised to 50. Each enquiry is undertaken by a group of between three and six members, who hear evidence from all interested parties. Press advertisements are used to invite evidence and reports are generally completed within three to six months, though more complex investigations sometimes take longer.

The MMC is concerned with three major types of enquiry:
- mergers;
- monopolies;
- anti-competitive practices.

These are discussed in Chapters 4, 5 and 6 respectively.

Table 1 The MMC's workload. Source: *MMC Annual Review 1989* (HMSO, 1990).

	1985	1986	1987	1988	1989
Mergers	4	6	6	4	13
Newspaper mergers	2	–	1	1	2
Monopolies	1	5	2	2	8
Competition	2	–	–	–	2
Public sector	4	3	3	4	3
General				1	
Labour					1
Airports			1		
Telecommunications					1
	13	14	13	12	30

Work on some reports will have been partly or wholly done in the previous year.

The Restrictive Trade Practices Court (**RTPC**)

Restrictive trade practices are agreements between firms concerning prices, output, or production processes. Such agreements came under the Restrictive Trade Practices Act, 1973, and it is a legal requirement that they are registered with the OFT.

The Court plays a role similar to that of the Monopolies and Mergers Commission in mergers and monopolies policies. However, its procedures differ from those of the MMC. The RTP is part of the legal system. It is headed by a judge, with seven lay members. It is also responsible for enforcing the ban on **resale price maintenance** (RPM) which prohibits firms from enforcing minimum prices for their products. The relevant legislation is the Resale Prices Act 1976. Suppliers can seek exemption from the ban on resale price maintenance from the RTP Court if they can prove that this is in the public interest; only books and pharmaceuticals have managed to gain an exemption. Like the MMC, the role of the RTPC is to investigate evidence submitted to it. Unlike the MMC, an adverse ruling by the RTPC is final, and does not require further action by the Secretary of State.

Specialized regulatory bodies

Privatization of public utilities in the 1980s has been accompanied by the growth of a series of specialized regulators responsible for individual industries. Examples are OFTEL, responsible for the telecommunications industry, OFGAS, OFWAT (water) and OFFER (electricity regulation). In general these are public utilities with a tendency towards natural monopoly, and they are generally dominated by a large former nationalized-industry company which could easily exploit a dominant position in the market. They occupy a central role in supplying factor inputs for the rest of the economy, so it is clearly in the **public interest** that they should operate as efficiently as possible.

For this reason, each regulator has its own full-time staff dedicated to the regulation of the industry concerned, rather than relying on a series of one-off investigations by the OFT staff. The role played by the regulatory body is similar to that of the Office of Fair Trading although on a continuous basis. The regulator monitors the price and output decisions of the industry, can conduct its own enquiry and negotiate with the industry to give undertakings on prices and competitive practices.

Like the OFT, the regulators have the back-up power to refer the industry to the Monopolies and Mergers Commission if an understanding cannot be reached. This reserve power acts as an incentive to the industry to conform to the regulator's proposal. If an MMC reference does take place, enquiry takes place in the normal way: reports go to the Trade Secretary, who will decide on action, as in the case of any other industry, in consultation with the regulator in this case. The regulator will be responsible for monitoring any undertakings or decisions required by the Secretary of State. The regulation of monopoly utilities raises a number of important competition policy issues which are examined in detail in Chapter 7.

Competition policy

UK competition policy procedures

The procedures for an EC investigation have already been outlined in the flow chart of Figure 5. Similar flow charts can be drawn up for UK procedures, as in Figures 6–8. The immediate point to note is that different procedures operate for each case: mergers, monopoly and anti-competitive practices, and restrictive practices. Although the actors are the same (the MMC and the RTPC playing the same parts) – the lines are subtly different in each case.

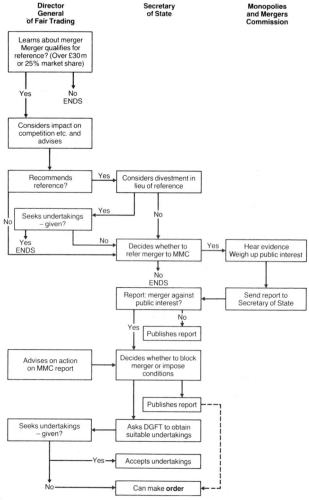

Figure 6 Mergers: who does what? Taken from *Competition Policy* published by the DTI

Mergers

Merger procedures are shown in Figure 6. In this case the DGFT *advises* on an MMC reference on the advice of the mergers panel, while the Trade Secretary makes the final *decision*. There are two clear-cut threshold points which must be passed before a reference is even considered:

- the merger must result in a group with a combined share of more than 25 per cent of the market; *or*
- the assets of the target firm exceed a certain value (£30 million in 1990).

The DGFT follows what have come to be called the **'Tebbit rules'**, laid down by the then Trade Secretary in 1984. These state that the criteria for investigation by the MMC are essentially confined to consideration of the effects of the merger on competition.

However, once the MMC investigation is undertaken, it must examine whether the merger will operate 'in the public interest'. The MMC's terms of reference therefore go beyond the 'Tebbit rules' under which the OFT operates. Five specific factors are identified in determining the public interest in Section 84 of the Fair Trading Act 1973, under which the MMC proceeds. These are: effective competition; consumer interests; innovation and new entry; the balanced distribution of industry and employment; and the international competitive position of UK producers.

Consideration of the last two factors could lead the MMC to conclusions different from those of the OFT. For example, regional considerations could prevent a merger which would not adversely affect competition, but would lead to the closing of a plant in an area of high unemployment. An MMC investigation therefore works in two stages: firstly, to establish whether a merger will reduce competition significantly; and then secondly, whether or not it is against the public interest. In effect the MMC adopts a case by case cost–benefit approach in its investigations, weighing up the balance of advantage and disadvantage of alternative arrangements from the overall viewpoint of the 'public interest'. This cost–benefit case-study method applies also to the MMC's approach to monopolies and anti-competitive practice enquiries, outlined below.

In order to decide whether competition will be adversely affected, an investigation by the MMC will examine a wide range of factors other than the size and market share. One obvious point is the ease with which new competitors could enter the market. If it is argued that the market *is* contestable, the OFT will require evidence that this is the case, and examine carefully any possible barriers to entry. Another factor is whether the product in question has any close substitutes. Competition from imports will also be taken into account.

Once the MMC reports, it is up to the Trade Secretary to decide whether to accept or reject the Commissions' recommendations. In practice, it is not unusual for the Trade Secretary to modify recommendations, but they are rarely rejected entirely. The OFT's function in obtaining compliance with decisions is also shown in Figure 6.

Monopolies and anti-competitive practices

The procedure for control of monopolies and anti-competitive practices is somewhat different from the procedures outlined above for control of mergers. The Director General of Fair Trading plays a rather greater role. The procedure is outlined in Figure 7. Where a monopoly (defined as 25 per cent of the market) already exists, the DGFT's powers include the ability to refer a case directly to the MMC. Note that this is different from the merger situation, where the DGFT can advise, but the MMC references are made by the Secretary of State for Trade and Industry. The MMC undertakes an investigation and then reports back to the Secretary of State, who again has ultimate powers of decision, advised by the OFT, in much the same way as in mergers policy.

The OFT has considerable powers to investigate and eliminate anti-competitive practices. As the flow chart shows, it is possible for the OFT to conduct its own enquiry, report on the existence of anti-competitive practices, and obtain undertakings to prevent further abuses. The whole process can be undertaken by the DGFT, acting independently, without reference to the Secretary of State, though normally there would be consultation between the DTI and the OFT.

In the case of anti-competitive practices, it is only where a firm fails to give satisfactory undertakings to the Office of Fair Trading that a Monopolies Commission reference is necessary. Reference to the MMC is therefore a sanction which the OFT can hold in reserve in negotiating with companies to ensure that no restraints of trade are operated. The threat of a reference to the Monopolies Commission puts considerable pressure on companies and organizations to conform to the OFT's recommendations. There are costs involved for companies which are referred to the MMC. Companies have the burden of providing data and information for an investigation. This occupies significant amounts of management time, and diverts them away from running their business. A Monopolies

UK competition policy in practice

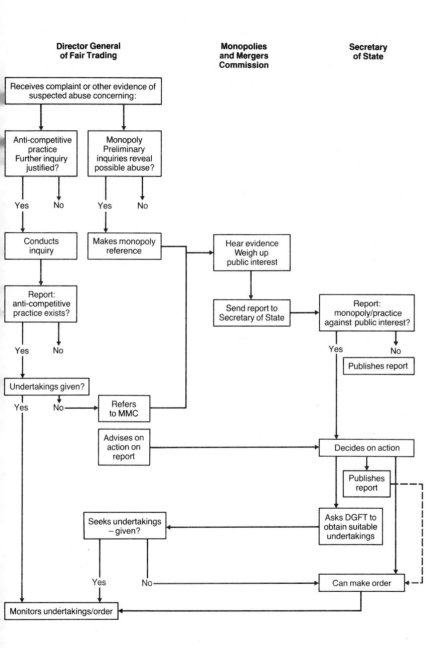

Figure 7 Monopolies and anti-competitive practices: who does what?
Taken from *Competition Policy* published by the DTI

Competition policy

Commission reference may generate unwelcome publicity for the company concerned. The deterrent effect of the threat of a referral to the MMC therefore allows the OFT to complete many of its investigations quite independently. Chapter 6 gives a number of examples of the operation of policy towards anti-competitive practices.

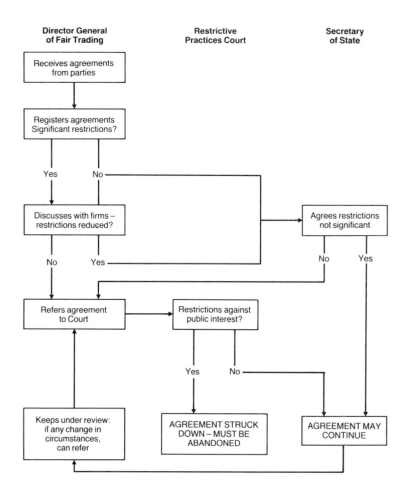

Figure 8 Restrictive trade practices: who does what? Taken from *Competition Policy* published by the DTI

Restrictive trade practices

Restrictive agreements concerning prices, output and production processes come under the Restrictive Trade Practices Act 1973, and it is a legal requirement that they are registered with the OFT. Regulation procedures are outlined in Figure 8. Again there are subtle differences from monopolies and mergers investigations. The RTPC takes an equivalent role to the MMC as investigatory body, though its procedures are different, as already noted, and the Secretary of State cannot amend the RTPC's decisions, unlike the preceeding cases.

There is another significant difference between the RTP legislation and the monopolies and mergers legislation. The **burden of proof** in monopoly and mergers enquiries is on the competition authorities, to demonstrate that the action is against the public interest. By contrast, the burden of proof in RTP legislation is on the firms, to demonstrate that the agreement is *not* against the public interest. All restrictive trade agreements must be registered by the firms with the OFT. It is not up to the OFT to make its own enquiries to find out what is going on, as is the situation in mergers and anti-competitive practices. Firms are legally obliged to inform the OFT by registration if they are undertaking any restrictive trade agreements.

Registered agreements are presumed to be against the public interest and are referred to the RTP unless they satisfy at least one of six conditions or **gateways.** The most significant gateways are: (a) that the restriction enables the public to receive specific and substantial benefits; and (b) that the agreement is necessary to prevent a serious and persistent adverse effect on the general level of unemployment. However, all agreements must pass the **tailpiece condition**: the benefits must outweigh the detriments from the agreements.

Since the RTP legislation first came into force in 1956 the vast majority of restrictive agreements have disappeared. There is strong evidence that prior to that date competition was significantly restricted. A major study of RTP by D. Swann and others, published in 1974, showed that of 2660 agreements registered between 1956 and 1969 only 370 were allowed to remain in place without amendment. In most cases prices fell sharply when an agreement was abandoned or disallowed by the RTP.

Up to 1968, 'information agreements' were permitted which allowed pre-notification of price rises between firms. This obvious invitation to concert price increases in an industry was then made illegal, and such schemes were replaced by post-notification agreements. Swann *et al.* noted that the abandoning of price agreements had the least effect where there were large firms which acted as significant 'price leaders' to the industry.

As noted above, the threat of a reference to the RTPC can be used by government as a bargaining counter, and can act as a powerful stimulus for change in this way. A most important example of this process was the case of the investigation of restrictive practices in the London Stock Exchange which ultimately led up to the reforms known as Big Bang in October 1987. In this case it was the threat of a reference to the Restrictive Practices Court of the Stock Exchange's rules which led to an agreement between the Trade Secretary and the Chairman of the Stock Exchange. Radical changes in the structure of the Stock Exchange led to the entry of large numbers of new firms into the market, and greatly increased competition. The result has been severe pressure on existing firms and new entrants' profit margins. Some of the firms which moved in when entry barriers were reduced have found that they cannot make an adequate return on their investments, and have had to withdraw. The competitive pressures evident since October 1987 are in marked contrast with the cosy world of fixed commissions and entry restrictions which preceded it.

Reform of competition policy

As the flow charts show, procedures vary quite considerably for different areas of competition policy. It is difficult to see the logic behind the separate existence and procedures of the RTPC, for example, and it is not clear why the DGFT should be able to refer monopoly cases to the MMC, without referring them to the Secretary of State, but not merger cases.

Reforms are in the pipeline which will move UK procedures more into line with the EC model outlined in Figure 5. In particular, it is likely that penalties for contravening competition law will be based on fines related to company turnover, rather than on the use of undertakings and court orders as at present, which is widely regarded as unsatisfactory.

Ideally a functional division of labour for competition policy should be possible. Where multinational firms are involved, competition policy issues need to be looked at from an international perspective, and the European Commission is probably most likely to provide this. In the UK, the OFT would have the function of market surveillance for infringements of any legislation, and for conducting preliminary investigations and negotiations with firms which appear to be acting anti-competitively. The DGFT should be able to refer references in all categories, including mergers, without having to act via the Secretary of State.

The MMC would perform the investigatory functions, as at present where an in-depth enquiry is felt to be necessary by the DGFT. It would cover all categories of enquiry, including restrictive practices. This would remove the anomaly of a courtroom approach of the RTPC, for which there is no obvious justification.

The Secretary of State would retain powers of final decision, as at present, once the MMC report was received. This would allow for political factors (the wider 'public interest') to be brought into consideration, if the government should decide that competition issues alone were not decisive. However, there seems little justification for political intervention in deciding which cases should be referred to the MMC, which remains true for mergers referrals under the present system. If the right to intervene in referrals is considered essential by governments, consistency suggests that this should be possible for all cases, not mergers alone.

KEY WORDS

European Commission	Compliance
Articles 85 and 86	Reference
Dominant position	RTPC
Regulatory capture	Resale price maintenance
Merger Control Regulation	Public interest
One–stop shopping	Tebbit rules
Regulatory bodies	Burden of proof
Director General of Fair Trading	Gateways
	Tailpiece conditions

Reading list

Crum, R. and Davies, S., Chapters 1 and 2 in *Multinationals*, Heinemann Educational, 1991.

Ferguson, P.R., 'The Monopolies and Mergers Commission and economic theory', *National Westminster Bank Quarterly Review*, Nov. 1985.

Fleming, M. and Swann, D., 'Competition policy – the pace quickens and 1992 approaches', *Royal Bank of Scotland Review*, June 1989.

Hill, B.E., Chapter 3 in *The European Community*, Heinemann Educational, 1991.

Hurl, B., *Privatization and the Public Sector*, Heinemann Educational, 1988, pp.47-48.

King, M. and Roell, A., 'The regulation of takeovers and the stock market', *National Westminster Bank Quarterly Review*, Feb. 1988.

Monopolies and Mergers Commission *Reviews* and Reports of the Director General of Fair Trading, both published annually by HMSO, are a good source of information on the current work of the Commission.

Paisley, R. and Quillfeldt, J., Chapter 31 in *Economics Investigated*, Collins Educational, 1989.

Essay topics

1. What are the arguments for the European Commission playing a role in competition policy, rather than leaving national governments entirely in charge of their own policies?
2. Explain why governments have pursued policies to regulate private monopolies. Consider the merits and demerits of a case by case approach to regulation as practised in the UK.
   [Welsh Joint Education Committee, 1990]
3. 'The central purpose of competition policy is to promote industrial efficiency through the identification and control of monopolies, cartels and other potential abuses of market power.' (C.M. Hardie). Discuss.
   [University of Oxford Local Examinations Syndicate, 1988]
4. Examine the statement 'The control of monopolies and restrictive practices should be relaxed in order to stimulate industrial expansion.'
   [Oxford and Cambridge Schools Examination Board, 1980]

Data Response Question 1
Concrete issues

This task is based on an examination question set by the University of London School Examinations Board in 1990. Read the extract, which is adapted from an article by A. Jackson in *The Times* of 13 February 1987, and answer the following questions.

1. Why should the author suggest that the abandonment of the cement cartel was 'a reluctant decision' of UK cement manufacturers?
2. How might the cement manufacturers have argued that the cartel was in the public interest?

3. Using appropriate diagram(s), analyse the factors which caused cement manufacturers to become 'vulnerable' after 1973.

Cement splits to face the frost of competition

One of the oldest cartels in the country has been disbanded leaving British cement manufacturers to fight it out. Blue Circle Industries (the market leader with 56.5 per cent of the market share), Rugby Portland Cement and Rio Tinto Zinc will now be able to charge variable prices throughout the country. This was a reluctant decision on the part of the cartel.

The common price agreement has been in existence since 1934, the firms maintaining that it was in the public interest for cement prices to be fixed countrywide. However, faced with a declining market after the construction industry peak in 1973, the major cement manufacturers were vulnerable. A major reason for the decline in the construction industry after 1973 was cuts in public expenditure. Thus, while gross domestic product rose by 16 per cent over the period 1973–85, output of the construction industry fell by 15 per cent. By the late 1970s our excess capacity in Britain was accompanied by a surplus in the rest of the world. The British market became a perfect target for importers.

Another development has been the growth in the use of substitute materials or extenders. Blast furnace slag and pulverised fuel ash are the two materials which can be blended successfully with ordinary Portland cement without impairing its cementitious properties.

Chapter Four
Monopoly policy

To be seriously rich, it helps to have ancestors who were in business before competition laws were developed.

A monopoly occurs when one firm is the sole producer of a good or service. In effect, the industry is one firm only. This is a straightforward case and is known as **simple monopoly**. We saw in Chapter 3 that as far as UK competition laws are concerned, a market share of 25 per cent is the 'trigger' which is actually used to consider whether a monopoly investigation should take place. To some extent a firm which is very large in relation to others in the industry may be able to act as a price leader, followed by the rest of the industry. This may enable it to restrict industry output 'as if' the whole industry is a monopoly. An alternative possibility is that a number of separate firms will act together to set prices and output, as if they are a profit-maximizing monopolist. In the UK an explicit or implicit **cartel** of this type is known as a **complex monopoly**. The MMC has been asked to investigate whether a complex monopoly has operated in several industries in recent years, including credit cards, brewing and petrol retailing. This chapter focuses initially on the standard case of single monopoly, and includes a discussion of complex monopolies and their implications for competition policy.

The causes of monopoly
Monopolies occur because of the existence of prohibitive **entry barriers**. In most industries there are barriers to entry of some sort. In monopoly, by definition, the barriers are high enough to deter any other entrants. We saw in Chapter 2 that price will be higher and output will be lower than in a competitive industry and 'super-normal' profits will occur, even in the long run (refer again to Figures 2 and 3).

Three types of entry barrier can be identified in principle: (i) legal entry barriers; (ii) innocent entry barriers; (iii) strategic entry barriers. In many monopolies a combination of these barriers operate.

Brewing as a Complex Monopoly

The Brewery industry in the UK was referred to the MMC in 1988. The British beer industry is unusual in that it is highly vertically integrated. British brewers make, distribute and retail beer. They own not only the breweries and the transport networks, but also the pubs in which the beer is sold. The MMC focused on the last point.

Seventy-five per cent of pubs in Britain are owned by a brewery, and 'tied' to taking all their supplies from the owning brewery. It is very difficult to obtain a licence to open a new pub, and the best sites are already taken. This means that the existing breweries can effectively prevent new entrants to the market. In practice, the commission concluded, they control the sales outlets. In some local areas all pubs are owned by the same brewery.

The MMC concluded that a complex monopoly did indeed exist, and was against the public interest. As evidence the MMC pointed to the rise in the price of beer, net of tax, by some 15 per cent in *real terms* between 1979 and 1987. They also noted the extraordinarily high prices being charged for soft drinks (orange juice frequently selling at above £3 per pint in 1988 prices, and Cola selling for more than beer, despite the absence of excise duty).

In order to increase competition by reducing entry barriers the MMC proposed that no single brewery should own more than 2000 pubs. All remaining tied pubs should be allowed to sell at least one 'guest beer', not brewed by the owner, and to buy soft drinks from any supplier.

However, the brewing industry can mount a powerful political lobby, and it is a large contributor to Conservative party funds. The Trade Secretary, Lord Young, decided after representations from the industry to modify the MMC's proposals (as we saw in Chapter 3, the Secretary of State is the ultimate decision-maker in monopolies investigations). The outcome was a compromise: instead of limiting each brewery to 2000 pubs, each was required only to sell *half* the excess over 2000 pubs owned.

Legal entry barriers
Legal entry barriers occur when a government grants a company monopoly powers by passing laws to ban other entrants to the same industry. There are three main reasons why this is done.

Revenue raising
In the past, valuable monopolies have been created by law in order to raise revenues for the government. A salt monopoly was used in fifteenth and sixteenth century England to increase Crown revenues. Today in Third World countries legal monopolies are still being created – particularly for imports – which are either sold to the highest bidder, or granted corruptly to supporters or relatives of political leaders. In a country where the tax collection system does not work, it may be easier to raise money by creating a monopoly. This may be inefficient, but there may be no better alternatives.

State-owned industries
In the UK, legal monopolies have often been granted to nationalized industries such as public utilities – electricity, gas, water, post and telecommunications. This has been done to prevent competitors entering small, highly profitable, segments of the industry, to leave the state-owned company to supply only the unprofitable business. This reasoning implies that the state companies were expected to cross-subsidize customers. Installing telephones in the Outer Hebrides presumably costs more than in central London, but for reasons of social policy consumers were charged the same amount. In the absence of legal restraints new entrants could perhaps offer a letter service in London only, at a price lower than the Post Office price, but not in the rest of the country; so legal barriers prevent 'cream-skimming', which could otherwise undermine the viability of the whole system. This is related closely to the existence of natural monopoly discussed below.

The patent system
The granting of a **patent** gives a firm a legal monopoly over the technology used to produce a good or service, for a limited time. The object of patents is to encourage research and development: if anyone could copy the results of R&D spending as soon as they appeared, it will be much cheaper to free-ride and copy than to undertake the initial research. Since this is true for everyone, there is a danger that, without patents, too little research would be undertaken. On the other hand, if patent protection is too strong,

excessive consumer exploitation by innovators could take place.

UK laws grant a patent for four years, after which it can be renewed annually up to a total of 20 years by paying fees. This may seem excessive, but in practice firms have to patent inventions before they are ready for production in order to safeguard them. The effective period of protection is generally less than this. In the meantime patents can be extremely valuable to the holders. The US Xerox corporation (Rank Xerox in the UK) held patents on photocopiers which for many years meant that it dominated the market and earned substantial profits. As these have expired, the market has become intensely competitive, and Xerox has had to fight to survive.

Companies may try to get round patents in order to enter a rich market by developing slightly different technologies to achieve the same objective. Polaroid corporation has held many key patents for 'instant-picture' photography. Kodak entered the market, but Polaroid sued Kodak, claiming that its patents had been infringed. The legal action in the US courts which followed was one of the most expensive in history, and ended with Kodak paying several hundred million dollars in damages when the courts found in Polaroid's favour.

There is plenty of room for debate as to how long patents should last, but most economists would accept that some legal protection of the results of research and development is necessary. The monopoly position established by patents is moderated by the provision that a patent holder is required to license the technology to anyone who wants to buy it for 'a reasonable fee'. What is reasonable is decided by arbitration, and makes for rich pickings for lawyers.

Innocent entry barriers

Innocent entry barriers occur as a side-effect of profit maximization. Once a firm is established in an industry, it may have certain advantages over potential entrants. In the case of a monopoly, these advantages may be prohibitive. The most general circumstance in which this is so is a **natural monopoly**.

A natural monopoly occurs when the total cost of supplying market demand is lower for one firm than it is for two or more firms. Figure 9 gives an example. AC is the cost curve faced by any firm. All producers are assumed to have identical costs. DD represents the market demand curve. If there is one firm in the market, 10 million units are sold at a cost of £10 per unit. If the same output

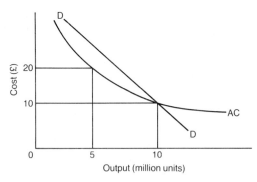

Figure 9 Illustrating the principle of a natural monopoly

were produced by two firms, each supplying 5 million units, the average cost would be £20 per unit. Clearly one firm can supply the market at lower cost than two firms. There are increasing returns to scale.

When the cost curve is as shown in Figure 9 the largest firm in the industry will have a cost advantage over its competitors and will sooner or later dominate the industry. Entrants will be deterred from coming in by the knowledge that they will suffer a cost disadvantage. They will particularly be deterred from entry where there are large **fixed costs** of production. When fixed costs are high, a firm needs to raise a large amount of money to enter the industry. In many cases, fixed costs are also **sunk costs**; that is to say, they cannot be recovered if a firm goes out of business. This acts as a further deterrent to entry. In the presence of sunk costs, there is a danger that a monopoly will be free from threat of entry even when it is inefficient. Potential entrants will be deterred from coming in by the fear of losing the value of their sunk investment costs in the event that entering the market ultimately proves unprofitable.

A natural monopoly is the clearest case of an innocent entry barrier, and as noted, where it does occur it is essential that some form of control is exercised to ensure that the advantages of cost reduction for consumers are not overwhelmed by monopolistic exploitation. In the UK this control has been implemented via nationalization up to the 1980s, and – following widespread privatization – by dedicated regulators, as discussed in Chapter 7.

There are other forms of innocent entry barrier, but for the most part these are not prohibitive and do not lead to pure monopoly. The exception is where a monopolist has control over sources of supply of a vital factor input. This *could* arise innocently but maintenance of such control is likely to involve strategic behaviour.

Strategic entry barriers

Strategic entry barriers occur where the incumbent firm deliberately undertakes behaviour which is explicitly designed to deter entry. Setting out to buy up or control all sources of supply amounts to a strategic barrier – even if a firm may have had an initially 'innocent' advantage in this respect. The world diamond market is a classic example. The De Beers Corporation has been able to monopolize the world diamond market because it owns the South African mines which account for the bulk of the world's output. It has strengthened its position by negotiating with other producers to join its central selling organization in a complex monopoly, in order to dominate the world market. This is a highly unusual case, in that the entire world market for a commodity is effectively monopolized.

Even cartels such as OPEC have been unable to operate a continuously effective complex monopoly in world markets, despite their powerful position, because they cannot control all the world's output.

Chapter 6 discusses a range of anti-competitive practices which are intended to increase entry barriers in order to protect the incumbent firm(s) from competition.

The accompanying newspaper article, which appeared as a leader in the *Financial Times*, 21 September 1990, discusses another form of entry barrier which has helped the world's airlines to maintain a complex monopoly against the threat of new entrants. Strategic behaviour is frequently used to defend a monopolistic position in more narrowly defined markets.

Entry barriers for airlines

COMPETITION in the airline industry depends on the ability of airlines to start operating any route if they so desire. But this ability is jeopardised by a system of allocating the capacity of airports that favours the incumbent. Airlines have property rights in the capacity – the "slots" – that they use at an airport, and the allocation of any surplus slots is managed by the airlines flying from that airport. Newcomers may be unable to gain access to a busy airport like Heathrow.

The European Commission has proposed that airlines which are not already operating from an airport at certain times, but which wish to do so, should have priority in the allocation of any slots which become available; and, if no slots become available after a year, established operators could be compelled to give up some slots.

This proposal implies a radical change in the present informal system: but changes have to be made. If competition is to develop in European scheduled services, airlines cannot go on agreeing how they share airport capacity. But the European Commission's proposals do not go far enough. They leave intact the curious system under which the airlines own the slots which they use, ownership which they have acquired simply by being there when the services began from that airport.

Allocating capacity

The normal method of allocating scarce capacity in a market economy is to sell it. For slots to be auctioned instead of shared would be a revolution for the airlines and would remove what they regard as one of their most valuable assets. But they are valuable because they give the airlines some control over the market; and the thrust of policy towards the airlines in Europe is to weaken this control.

More slots

If slots were sold, airlines would pay what they were worth to them. Entrants would be able to get slots when they wanted them, up to the number they thought worth buying.

Incumbents might seek to bid up prices to discourage new competitors; some regulators fear that richer airlines could exploit their strength to push up prices beyond the means of newcomers. But their ability to do so would depend on the effectiveness of their efforts to maintain monopoly power on some parts of their network.

The problem is one of preventing the acquisition of monopoly power by airlines or regulating its use. It is an argument for promoting competition and regulating monopolies, not an argument against the use of market forces. The Commission's proposals should be regarded as a step towards more radical changes.

The value of a monopoly

A monopoly is only worth having if it is profitable. Whether or not it is profitable depends on two factors; the elasticity of demand for the product, and the cost of producing it. If the government granted you a legal monopoly over the supply of solid gold door handles, your fortune would not be made. Given the cost of production, the demand simply does not exist. There are plenty of more realistic examples. British Rail's Network South East commuter services have a monopoly of rail transport, and might be expected to be highly profitable. Yet despite the fact that demand elasticity is quite low, owing to the relative lack of substitutes available, the services have consistently lost money. The operating costs of the system are very high. The monopoly is not a licence to print money. Similarly, for many years British Coal had a legal monopoly over coal production in the UK, yet it still lost money consistently.

On the other hand, monopolies can be sources of immense wealth. The riches of the Rockefellers came from John D. Rockefeller's successful monopolization of the US oil industry by the creation of the Standard Oil Company in the late nineteenth century. The US Anti-Trust (anti-monopoly) laws were a direct response, and led to the break-up of the company, though not before the family had amassed a huge fortune. To be seriously rich it helps to have ancestors who were in business in the days before competition laws were developed. 'Hot Gossip' on the following page provides a striking example.

A monopoly can exist on a *local, national* or *international* level. At the local level, strategic behaviour can result in very profitable monopolies. Any industry where success depends on access to a prime site is vulnerable to monopolization. Although food retailing is generally speaking highly competitive, local monopolies can and do exist in areas where prime sites are restricted, owing to the operation of planning laws. If a company manages to obtain a key site for a superstore in a congested area, rivals face prohibitive entry barriers. Most national supermarket chains operate two or even three different price lists for identical goods in their stores, depending on their location. Where local competition is high, the lowest list operates, and vice versa. Similar factors operate in the case of local bus services (see Chapter 6), and the beer market (see later in this chapter).

The regulation of monopolies

Government policy towards monopolies falls into two distinct areas, simple monopolies and complex monopolies. As we have already seen, competition policy sets out to ensure that monopolies are only allowed to exist if it can be demonstrated that their forma-

Competition policy

> ## HOT GOSSIP
>
> Gloria TNT, and her husband, Prince Johannes von Thurn und Taxis, are no ordinary couple. He is one of the richest men in Europe, and the German popular press cannot get enough of him. Before he could inherit, he had to have an heir. So a few years ago, he married. His wife is 29 and known, naturally enough, as Gloria TNT. They have three small children, including a son, Johannes.
>
> The TNTs' lives keep a battery of gossip columnists in jobs. Last February they fed eagerly off the Princess' legal battle with the designer who tried selling gold-coloured hot pants bearing her name. Not only did he rip her off, he gave away a free condom with each sale. Just a month ago, Prince Johannes was reportedly upset by his wife's growing interest in another Prince, the pop star, who featured heavily at a party she gave at Munich's trendy Parkcafe.
>
> The Prince's riches, estimated at up to $3 billion, came from the *family monopoly of the postal system* throughout continental Europe. By 1867, when the monopoly was finally broken up, it had netted them enough to build a house twice as large as Buckingham Palace, to buy more than 60,000 acres of romantic German woodland, a 150,000 acre farm in Brazil, a chunk of the Bayerische Vereinsbank and holdings in brewing, commercial property and industry.
>
> Source: *Independent on Sunday*, 12 August 1990

tion will not operate against the public interest. This means that in practice very few straightforward 'simple' monopolies exist, other than public utilities. Regulation of public utilities and former state monopolies is discussed in Chapter 7.

Much of the MMC's work concerning monopolies therefore deals with complex monopoly issues. In recent years there have been a number of references of industries in which it was suspected that complex monopolies were operating. Not surprisingly, these were difficult and complicated investigations, where it was hard for the commission to establish conclusively whether or not *de facto* monopolies were actually operating.

One immediate problem facing regulators is how to identify the *existence* of a complex monopoly. It is often suggested that if firms all charge the same price, and tend to change prices at the same time, then this is evidence of collusion and a complex monopoly must exist. Consumers are always deeply suspicious that petrol prices, for example, are being rigged by a cartel of oil companies. The MMC has been called in to investigate petrol retailing on several occasions.

However, any industry which is highly competitive will show symptoms with regard to price levels and changes which are

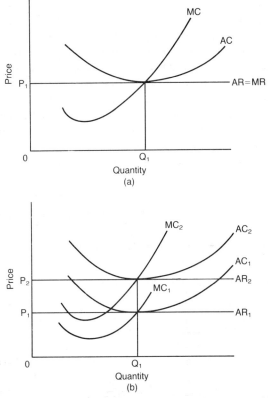

Figure 10 (a) Equilibrium price and output for perfect competition. All firms are price-takers at a price P_1. (b) Effects of a cost increase. The upwards shift in the AC curve results in all cost increases being passed on to consumers

identical to those of a complex monopoly. To take the extreme case of perfect competition, every student knows that firms face a perfectly elastic demand curve – they are **price takers**. In other words, firms have no option but to charge the market price. They cannot charge more – because they will lose all their customers to rival firms. It is not worth charging less, because they will then not make **normal profits** (see Chapter 2), and it will not be worthwhile to stay in business. And if costs increase, then in a perfectly competitive market, price will have to increase for all firms – at the same time. Figure 10 illustrates this.

Since price movements in both complex monopoly and perfect competition will look exactly the same, the MMC will need to investigate thoroughly to establish the existence or otherwise of monopoly. It generally focuses closely on rates of return in the industry in order to establish whether profit levels appear to be excessive. Again there are obvious difficulties. Normal profits do vary between competitive industries, depending on how risky they are. Rates of return on capital of computer firms are likely, on the average, to be higher than those of food retailers. Food retailing is generally a low-risk, stable industry, compared with computing. To establish what is a 'reasonable' rate of return for petroleum retailing, a view has to be taken by the commission on the riskiness of the business. Similar problems arose in the case of the brewing industry, which is examined in the accompanying article from *The Times* of 11 July 1989.

Big brewers will not be forced to sell off pubs

Britain's biggest breweries are to retain the ownership of their public houses despite a Monopolies and Mergers Commission recommendation that they should be ordered to sell 22,000 of them.

In a move to bring greater competition they are being forced to allow 11,000 of their premises to become free houses.

The big six – Allied Lyons, Bass, Courage, Grand Metropolitan, Scottish and Newcastle, and Whitbread – are to be required to lease out half of the pubs that they own above a threshold of 2000.

And in a move to encourage cheaper soft drinks and low alcohol beers, tenants of the national brewers are to be allowed to buy those and other products from any source. Tenants of the national brewers will also be allowed to stock a "guest" beer.

The compromise on the future of the beer industry was announced by Lord Young of Graffham, Secretary of State for Trade and Industry, amid charges that he had surrendered to the interest of the big brewers. Mr Bryan Gould, shadow trade and industry secretary, called it a "craven and complete capitulation".

The Brewers' Society said it regretted the decision, which would be damaging for consumers, while the Consumers' Association accused the Government of failing to break the big brewers' stranglehold over the supply of beer.

In a statement, it said it opposed the free house proposals and "regretted that Lord Young has chosen to repeat his idea that the national brewers should operate many of their pubs on an arm's-length basis. This will be extremely difficult to put into effect and will be detrimental to both consumers and tenant licensees."

The Consumers' Association said the changes were a "disappointing compromise". It added: "The big brewers have got off lightly and the regional brewers have got off scot free."

It remained to be convinced whether prices would come down or that drinkers would have a better choice.

The big six own three out of four pubs and account for 75 per cent of beer production. There will now be an additional 11,030 free houses to the existing 15,000.

Lord Young's decision is a significant retreat from the recommendations of the Monopolies and Mergers Commission, which proposed in March that no brewer should be allowed to own more than 2000 licensed premises.

Philip Webster

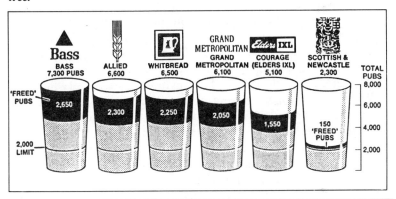

KEY WORDS	
Simple monopoly	Natural monopoly
Cartel	Fixed costs
Complex monopoly	Sunk costs
Entry barriers	Price takers
Patent	Normal profits

Reading list

Barker, 'Competition from new entrants', in *Case Studies in the Competitive Process*, Heinemann Educational Books, 1976.

Bloor, I. and Cockerill, A., 'Competition and the UK brewing industry', *Economic Review*, Jan. 1989.

Burningham, D. (ed.), 'Markets and efficiency', in *Understanding Economics*, Hodder & Stoughton, 1990.

Chiplin, B. and Wright, M., Chapters 3 and 7 in *The Logic of Mergers*, IEA, 1987.

Greenaway, D. and Reed, G., 'Price discrimination and airline tickets', *Economic Review*, Sept. 1988.

Harris, J. and Janes, E., *Economics Data Response Questions Answered* (chap. 2, no. 2), Pitman, 1989.

Paisley, R. and Quillfeldt, J., Chapter 19 in *Economics Investigated*, Collins Educational, 1989.

Williams, G., 'Achieving a competitive environment for Europe's airline industry', *National Westminster Bank Quarterly Review*, May 1990.

Essay topics

1. What is the difference between 'innocent' and 'strategic' entry barriers? Is the difference significant for competition policy?
2. What is meant by barriers to entry into an industry? What implications do they have for the profits earned by firms and the use of efficient methods of production?
   [University of Oxford Local Examinations Syndicate, 1988]
3. What factors might cause a change in the prices charged by a firm for its products? What implications does the degree of competition have?
   [University of Oxford Local Examinations Syndicate, 1989]
4. Explain what is meant by monopoly profits? What reasons are there for believing that a monopoly agreement between a number of firms may be more harmful than a single firm monopoly, from society's point of view? Why does the state grant monopoly rights in the form of patents to particular firms?
   [Welsh Joint Education Committee, 1989]

Data Response Question 2

Bad dreams for the motor trade

Read the accompanying article by John Griffiths from the *Financial Times* of 10 May 1990, and answer the following questions.

1. In which two countries are car prices highest in the EC: (a) net of tax, and (b) after new car taxes? Which two countries have the lowest new car taxes? Which two countries have the highest?
2. Using supply and demand diagrams, suggest why countries with high taxes tend to have low prices net of tax, according to the chart.

3. Why does the existence of large differences in prices net of tax between countries suggest that monopolistic or anti-competitive practices are operating in some countries (such as the UK)?
4. What evidence would the MMC examine to establish the existence of a complex monopoly in the UK car market? Would you expect the European Commission to play any role in investigating the car market? What factors determine whether this is a matter for the EC or for the MMC? (Note that this MMC reference took place before the implementation of the EC's new Merger Control Regulation, in September 1990.)

Bad dreams return to the motor trade

YESTERDAY'S referral of UK new car prices to the Monopolies and Mergers Commission is a five-year-old bad dream come back to give motor manufacturers and dealers sleepless nights.

It is certain to generate a wave of suspicion and cynicism among British consumers – and not just about the prices they are charged both for cars and the parts that keep them on the road.

The announcement of the referral by Sir Gordon Borrie, Director General of Fair Trading, must also cast renewed doubt on the efficacy of the European Community rules put in place at the end of 1984 with the intention of protecting consumers' interests.

Consumers' associations, not least the Brussels-based Bureau European des Unions de Consommateurs, waged a publicity war in the early to mid 1980s to convince motorists in the UK and some other EC countries that they were being charged much higher prices than were warranted because manufacturers were taking advantage of outdated customs and perceptions of "what the market will bear."

They were being helped in keeping prices high, the consumer groups argued, by such devices as restrictions on Japanese car imports in some markets (to a ceiling of 11 per cent of new car sales in the UK) and the refusal of dealers in countries where cars were cheap – under pressure from their suppliers – to supply them to motorists wanting to import them into high-priced markets.

Over several years the manufacturers fought a fierce rear-guard action in which they claimed that cross-border price differentials were much less than claimed.

Differential taxation regimes, exchange rate variations, and even the existence of different specifications in individual markets were all arguments used by the manufacturers in an effort to convince buyers that there were no "rip-offs".

John Griffiths

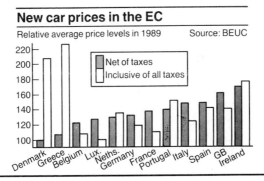

New car prices in the EC
Relative average price levels in 1989   Source: BEUC

Chapter Five
Mergers policy in the UK

The financial press likes a good story, and the emergence of financial supermen makes for an interesting read. Inflated reputations and egos are only too easy to acquire.

This chapter examines UK policies towards corporate mergers. We have seen in Chapter 2 the theoretical case against market dominance. Mergers which result in the creation of full or partial monopolies are an obvious way in which such dominance can be achieved, at least in the short run. In Chapter 3 we examined the role of the European Commission and the UK regulatory bodies in competition policy. We now look more closely at policy towards mergers. The chapter starts with a brief review of the level of merger activity in Britain, and the pattern that mergers have taken. We then examine the economics of mergers, and look at the arguments for and against government intervention into the mergers market. In the process we examine the argument that financial markets in the English-speaking economies take an unduly short-term view of profits, which results in excessive takeover activity at the expense of long-term performance. We conclude with an evaluation of possible reforms of the competition policy process.

Categories of mergers
Three distinct **types of merger** may be distinguished: horizontal, vertical and conglomerate.

Horizontal mergers
Horizontal mergers occur when two companies producing the same product in the market come together. If Sainsbury merged with Tesco, for example, this would create a food retailer with a substantial share of the UK market, and the possibility of higher food prices arising from that dominant market position. As we have seen, this is by no means certain, since it depends very much on the existence of barriers to prevent the entry of new competitors to the market. As a general principle, it is easy to see that horizontal mergers pose at least a threat of limiting competition and the establishment of domi-

nant market share. On the other hand, they may yield economies of scale which result in lower costs and improvements in resource allocation. If above the 25 per cent market share or £30 million size limit, then there is a case for OFT or MMC investigation.

Vertical mergers

Mergers may result in the vertical integration of two companies, where a company takes over an actual or potential supplier or customer. For example, British Airways might attempt to take over the British Airports Authority, who run the major UK airports. In cases like this, market share cannot be used as a criterion for investigation, since neither firm's share of its market will be directly affected by the merger. British Airways' share of the airline market would not change, nor would the BAA's share of the UK market for aircraft landings and take-offs, as a result of the merger. However, the OFT would consider the risk that opportunities for competitors might be jeopardized by the merger. Clearly this would be a considerable risk in this hypothetical example. The airline could ensure that its flights received the most desirable time slots or even exclude competition altogether from the major UK airports. Similar considerations might apply in the case of mergers between a brewery and a hotel company. The brewery could obtain sole access for its own products in the hotel group, excluding other competitors from supply. The key economic issue that must be addressed is the extent to which alternative sources of supply or alternative customers exist within a market. In our examples there would be an initial case for investigation. In the first example, there are few if any alternatives to BAA airports for other airlines. In the second the hotel group could own important sites for which in practice there is limited local competition, so that competing brewers would find it difficult to find alternative sales outlets.

Conglomerate mergers

A conglomerate merger occurs when two companies which supply unrelated goods and/or services merge. In this case there is no direct effect on competition. The Office of Fair Trading suggests a number of ways in which large diversified groups may behave in ways that have detrimental effects on competition. These include cross-subsidizing activity from revenue generated elsewhere, lack of pressure to innovate and compete aggressively in selling its product, and undertaking internally financed investment at lower than market rates of return.

At first sight there seems no reason why any of these factors should be of concern to the public interest, though clearly they would matter to the shareholders of the companies concerned. The real competition policy issues that do arise in conglomerate mergers concern problems of the size of the newly merged groups. Large size raises the possibilities of predatory pricing and vertical restraints on trade. These are discussed in detail in Chapter 6.

The merger boom

The late 1980s saw a rapid increase in both the number and value of mergers taking place, as Figure 11 shows. Before then, distinct 'peaks' in merger activities occurred in 1968 and 1972, with relatively lower levels of activity during the remainder of the 1970s and early 1980s. Recently there has been a very high level of merger activity, as the chart shows; and although a slowdown has occurred

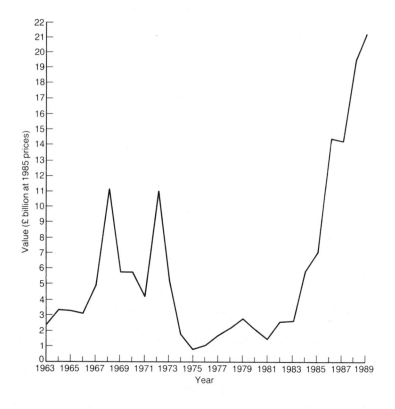

Figure 11 UK aquisitions and mergers

in 1990, a glance at the *Financial Times* shows that almost every day some sort of deal is announced.

In the 1960s, the government's attitude towards mergers was ambivalent. Although the MMC continued to operate, the government also promoted some industrial mergers in the belief that economies of scale were vital for British companies to be competitive in international markets. The Industrial Reorganization Corporation (IRC) was set up to promote mergers. The policy was summarized sceptically as: 'In order to achieve industrial efficiency, find the most efficient firm in Britain and merge the rest into it.'

The IRC's efforts provide an illustration of the problems of government intervention into the structure of industry. Regardless of theoretical possibilities, several of the IRC's constructions ran into grave difficulties which, in some cases at least, appeared to be a direct result of the ill-judged nature of the mergers themselves.

The UK car industry provides a notable and unfortunate example. A series of mergers brought together the British Motor Corporation (Austin plus Morris) with Jaguar, Triumph and Rover, all under the management of the Leyland Truck Company. Whereas the Leyland management had apparently made a good job of producing heavy lorries, the task of rationalizing the separate components of the UK industry into a coherent unit proved beyond their capabilities. The group's performance after the merger was by any standards an unmitigated disaster. Only in the late 1980s, after a series of massive subsidies and the large scale running down of capacity, was a return to viability possible. This was achieved in effect by unscrambling the original merger and selling off the surviving sections of the original company separately.

Few of the IRC's offspring performed any better. Even the GEC–AEI merger in the electrical industry, which was the one notable success in the 1970s, was criticized in the 1980s for sacrificing long-term investment policy to short-term financial performance.

The IRC's strategy of **picking winners** to act as national champions in international markets influenced the climate of opinion towards mergers. There was in any case a trend towards comglomerate mergers which developed during the 1960s and 1970s. In many cases the industrial logic or economic rationale of these mergers was difficult to discern. The result was the creation of some large and difficult to manage companies which performed notably less successfully after merger than they had done as separate units.

From the beginning of the 1980s there were an increasing number of company transactions which were in effect **de-mergers**. The severe recession of 1980–82 led to many large industrial companies either going out of business completely, or selling off subsidiaries of their business. There was an increasing number of **management buy-outs** (see Chapter 2). Since the subsidiaries were often loss-making, the price was low, but the risks were high. Freed from control by a bureaucratic head office, some MBOs have been very successful; others have collapsed under the burden of excessive debt and over-optimistic growth forecasts.

The merger boom in the late 1980s did differ significantly from the merger waves in the 1960s and 1970s. There were still examples of big 'textbook' mergers in which the bidders' motives were increased economies of scale or marketing, or attempts to increase market power. The Nestlé acquisition of Rowntree Mackintosh in the confectionary market is an example. But in many other takeover bids the chief objective was to unscramble some of the ill-advised conglomerate mergers that had occurred in the preceding decades. The statistics show a series of massive 'merger' transactions as companies were bought and sold. But in fact some of the largest bids in recent years have been undertaken by **corporate raiders** such as Hanson Trust and BTR, their objective being to break up companies which had performed poorly in the aftermath of previous mergers. Much of the apparent increase in merger activity results from secondary transactions that take place after a major bid has succeeded, as the bidder breaks up the target company and re-sells the components.

The activities of corporate raiders are highly controversial. Opponents object to so-called **asset-stripping** in which plants are shut down and jobs lost in order to redevelop commercial property. Subsidiaries are traded back and forth between companies with apparently little or no regard for the welfare of the employees.

Free-market supporters of the takeover specialists argue that they perform an essential function in improving the efficiency and competitiveness of companies that would be destined for failure anyway, with even worse consequences. The argument that threat of takeover concentrates the minds of managements everywhere is also put forward.

There is something in both of the arguments. When the general level of unemployment in the economy is high, the short-term social costs of job losses due to restructuring are severe. On the other hand, when the economy is prospering, closing down factories in labour-shortage areas such as the South East and transferring production to other parts of the country, where factor inputs are more readily available and cheaper, makes economic sense. Valuable sites are redeveloped, and there is no real shortage of jobs available for those made redundant in the South East.

Contested versus agreed mergers

In the UK it is takeover bids that generally make the headlines. In a takeover there is a battle for control of the target company; this is known as a **contested bid**. The existing management (the incumbents) try to convince the shareholders not to sell their shares to the bidder. Takeover battles are very common in countries where the stock market is an important source of company finance (notably the UK and the USA, and other English-speaking countries). In other countries, where stock markets play a smaller role, and the banks provide most of the captial for company finances, contested bids are practically non-existent.

In Germany and Japan, although mergers do take place, they are almost always **agreed mergers** between the managements of the two companies concerned. The directors of the target company advise shareholders to accept the offer being made by the bidder. Many mergers take place on an agreed basis in the UK and the USA, as well as the more publicized takeover battles.

From the viewpoint of competition, it makes no difference how the merger takes place. What matters is how competition is affected by the merger. However, there may be a case for government control of mergers if it can be shown that merger activity is in some sense 'excessive'.

Should we have a mergers policy?

Our discussion so far has already suggested arguments for and against government intervention into the mergers process. These can be summarized as follows:

Against intervention

- Mergers result in *economies of scale*, and therefore improved resource allocation.
- Contested takeovers mean that efficient managements are able to take over assets that inefficient managements are not using effectively. *Survival of the fittest* ensures efficiency.
- The market will sort out mistakes. If unsuccessful mergers occur, corporate raiders are always ready to boot out the unsuccessful management and unscramble the merger.
- Even if markets occasionally fail, government intervention is even more of a failure in practice.

In favour of intervention

- Mergers create monopolies; consumers are exploited by monopolies, and resources misallocated.
- On the average there is no evidence that mergers improve companies' performance, either in terms of profitability, or resource allocation.
- The huge fees earned by advisors and shareholders in takeover battles result in 'excessive' merger activity. Insider dealing and business corruption are encouraged.
- Takeover bids are disruptive. Managers spend far too much time concocting bids, or defence against bids. They end up neglecting the fundamentals of their business and company performance suffers as a result.

The first points for and against – economies of scale versus monopolistic exploitation – have been covered in Chapters 2 and 4. As we have seen, the role of investigations by the OFT and MMC is in effect to weigh these conflicting considerations and come to a decision concerning the balance of advantage and disadvantage.

The second points for and against can also be taken together. It can certainly be argued that there is no convincing evidence that mergers *in general* have improved resource allocation. If this is so, why not ban them altogether once they reach the threshold rules (in the UK, 25 per cent of the market or over £30 million)?

Defenders of mergers point to the structure of ownership of UK industry. Most large firms in Britain are owned by **institutional shareholders,** such as pension funds or insurance companies. They hold shares to provide investment income, out of which they pay out their obligations to pensioners or policy holders. Even Britain's largest institutional investor, the Prudential Insurance Company, generally restricts its holdings to around 5 per cent of the total value of any one company, to diversify its investments.

This means that there is a **divorce of ownership from control.** The owners of large companies generally do not manage them. Professional managers' interests may not be the same as the shareholders' main interest, the profitability of the company. Managers may be more concerned with maximizing their own income and welfare, rather than that of the shareholders.

The existence of an active **market for corporate control** may be the only effective discipline to ensure that shareholders' interests are safeguarded. Dissatisfied shareholders really only have one practical option – to sell their shares and buy elsewhere. If enough do, a depressed share price will attract corporate raiders.

The threat of a **hostile takeover** puts pressure on the existing management to make sure that they do not fall too far behind the standards of financial performance being achieved elsewhere in the industry. Directors will lose their jobs as well as control of the company. Corporate raiders keep dozy managements on their toes. Even if in fact there are relatively few contested mergers, the threat of takeover concentrates the minds of managements. Even if there is no evidence that takeovers do actually result in more efficient use of resources, predators should still be allowed to roam.

In order to examine the third point for intervention – that there is excessive and unwarranted merger activity – it is worth looking more closely at the causes of some of the frenzied merger booms that have occurred in the past.

One explanation is based on the bahaviour of monetary policy. The argument is that a **bull market** (a stock market boom) is often due to lax monetary conditions. A rapidly expanding money supply and 'low' interest rates are indications that monetary policy is excessively expansionary. Much of the increased credit finds its way into the stock market, and bids up share prices speculatively. At first the share price rise appears to be justified by the bright earnings prospects of companies, since demand is strong, and sales are high. Eventually it becomes clear that the situation is inflationary, and rapid output growth cannot be sustained indefinitely.

While expansion is taking place, with interest rates low, there are generous funds available in the financial system to finance increased takeover activity. Banks and investment advisers earn large fees from advising companies in mergers. Companies will find themselves contacted with proposals for acquisitions to expand their business. The temptation may be great. Sales are expanding rapidly. It may seem cheaper, and it is certainly quicker, to expand productive capacity by buying a rival company than by investing in internal growth. It may also be possible to acquire a degree of monopolistic market power by acquisition.

During a boom period, some managements may be deluded into believing that the rapidly increasing profitability of their company is due to their own exceptional managerial talents, rather than the short-lived and unsustainable boom conditions. At such times there will be no shortage of advisers anxious to earn fees and commissions to reinforce such views. The financial press likes a good story, and the emergence of financial supermen makes for an interesting read. Inflated reputations and egos are only too easy to acquire.

Once on the growth-by-acquisition path it may be difficult to get off.

Profits growth should be satisfactory while the boom lasts. However, to support an inflated share price which is discounting future growth, future acquisitions may be necessary. At some point the bubble bursts as monetary conditions tighten. If the companies have been reasonably well managed, the worst that will happen is a sharp fall in the share price. But if management effort has been directed at financial dealing rather than running the company, and acquisition has resulted in heavy debt interest costs, the result will be a collapse. The accompanying article from the *Independent on Sunday* of 12 August 1990 illustrates just how quickly and severely collapse can occur: virtually every company cited in the list had been involved heavily in mergers and acquisitions during the 1980s.

Slump exposes glaring errors

THE ECONOMIC slowdown is ripping open the cracks in British management skills. An analysis of 1990's biggest stock market losers shows clearly that the majority are companies that made one or more disastrous decisions during the 1980s, writes David Bowen.

There is a concentration in certain sectors. Eight of the 30 companies that lost at least half their value are in property or construction: Fairbriar, Penant, Cabra, Rush & Tompkins (in receivership), McCarthy & Stone, Dares, London and Metropolitan and Sheraton Securities. Five – VPI, Parkway, Saatchi & Saatchi, Carlton Communications, TVS – are related to the media and have been hit by the biggest slump in advertising since the early 1970s. Others, such as Coloroll, the collapsed home furnishings group, and Pepe, which makes jeans, have been damaged by the fall in consumer spending.

But a much clearer theme, affecting about half the companies, is overambition: the problems of Coloroll, VPI, Astra, Kelt Energy, International Business Communications and FKB can be pinned mainly on acquisitions that went wrong. Other expansion difficulties ranged from LIT's risky foray into financial futures clearing, via Parkfield's disastrous attempt to grow rapidly in video distribution, to Hunterprint's poorly managed move to a new factory.

There are inevitably some bad luck stories. Erskine House, which distributes office equipment, is a fast-growing group that disappointed the City by losing momentum. But the root of its current problems lies in *perestroika*. Its partners in the Soviet Union could not cope with the new pressures, and withdrew from the business. Defence companies are not the only ones to suffer from the changes in Eastern Europe.

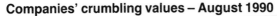

Mergers policy in the UK

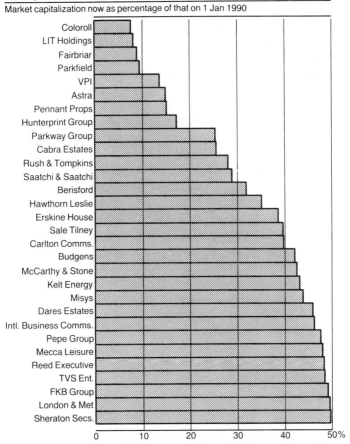

Companies' crumbling values – August 1990

Market capitalization now as percentage of that on 1 Jan 1990

A related explanation of merger booms is that the stock market fails to value the riskiness of different companies accurately. In boom conditions, when share prices are rising rapidly, the risk of financial collapse is low. 'High-risk' companies will tend to be making particularly good profits at this stage of the cycle, and there is a good chance that, in the euphoria of a bull market, their shares will be bid up beyond their long-run 'equilibrium' value. By contrast, more conservative and stolid companies will tend to under-perform the market at this stage of the cycle. Managers of the 'glamour' companies may well be tempted to take advantage of the excessive gap that opens up between the ratings of glamour stocks and more conservatively managed companies. The bull market's appetite for new share issues also induces opportunistic bids before a **market correction** takes place, as it usually does.

Short-termism

The agreement is that there is too much pressure for short-term results, and not enough emphasis on less glamorous but ultimately more successful long-term investment in improving product quality. Institutional investment fund managers are under pressure to purchase rapid increases in asset values – and they will be tempted to accept a takeover bid for a quick profit, even if it looks unlikely to improve the real performance of the companies involved. Critics argue that the stock markets of the UK, the USA and Australia are dominated by damaging **short-termism**, in contrast to the longer-term view taken by investors in continental Europe and Japan.

To the extent that this characterization is correct – and undoubtedly it contains elements of truth – there is a case for government intervention. However, it is not a competition policy issue. The issue is whether the interests of managements or shareholders need to be protected in a market that is functioning imperfectly. This brings us back to the fundamental question involved in all regulation, discussed in Chapter 4. Will government intervention, in practice, prove to be more efficient than letting the market sort its own mistakes out, as the demerger processes taking place in the 1980s perhaps suggests? Markets are imperfect – but government intervention may also be imperfect.

Current mergers policy

Clearly there are powerful arguments both for and against active government intervention in the mergers process. Current government policy has been discussed in Chapter 3. Essentially, intervention into mergers occurs only if there is a threat to competition both at the EC level (merger control regulation) and in the UK (the Tebbit rules). It is not regarded as an appropriate role for government to make any judgements as to whether a particular merger will result in greater or lesser efficiency. If it turns out to be a disaster, that is a matter for the shareholders, not the government. The market will sort out problems eventually, and government is unlikely to do any better.

However, it is accepted that governments have a duty to ensure 'fair play', and that insider dealing and fraud are prevented. The

Guinness trial of 1990 showed the extent to which a successful management could become corrupted into a win-at-all-costs approach.

Ernest Saunders, former Chairman of Guinness, painted a lurid picture at his trial in 1990 of merchant banks and financial advisors bombarding him with proposals for bids for company after company. Saunders claimed that these advisors pushed aggressively to get takeovers under way because of the massive fees they would earn from bids.

Is there a case, then, for trying to discourage – or at least slow down – the level of merger activity? If current arrangements do result in excessive activity, some critics argue that we should in effect change the rules in order to make it more difficult for mergers to take place: we should 'throw sand into the merger machine'. A number of proposals have been made:

(1) We should require that shareholders in the *bidding* company must vote on whether to approve a takeover proposal by their management.
(2) We should require all companies to include a majority of **non-executive** ('independent') **directors** on their boards.
(3) We should require that the threshold beyond which large shareholders are required to bid for the whole company be reduced from 29.9 to 14.9 per cent (preventing predators building up a strong position before making a bid).
(4) We should extend the 'bid period' under the takeover rules to allow more time for examining and analysing the logic of bids.
(5) We should delay the transfer of voting rights on large share stakes until some time after purchase.
(6) We should impose a **moratorium** (delay) **rule**, prohibiting anyone who buys a given percentage of the shares from mounting a takeover for a number of years (generally three to five years), unless the existing board approves.
(7) We should replace the annual shareholders meeting with five-yearly reviews of executive performance in meeting long-term objectives.
(8) Contested takeovers should be banned altogether.

Items (1)–(4) in the above list would act to strengthen the rights of shareholders. However, items (5)–(8) would effectively strengthen management powers, at the potential expense of shareholders. Bad managements could shelter behind a wall of takeover barriers, and shareholders' powers to change a management team would be significantly reduced.

The dilemma for policy-makers is to strike a balance between two conflicting aims: on the one hand, the avoidance of an excessively short-term approach to financial performance which distracts managements away from improving their products; and on the other hand, making sure that inefficient managements can be effectively disciplined by the threat of takeover.

Conclusions

This chapter has reviewed the pattern of mergers in the UK, and examined the case for and against government intervention in the mergers process. The competition policy arguments for merger control are quite straightforward. They suggest that mergers policy should simply be an extension of the monopolies policy outlined in Chapter 4. If a proposed merger will result in market dominance, and if there are significant entry barriers which inhibit the development of competiton, mergers should be banned. In other cases, the government should refrain from intervening in the market for corporate control, which is a useful mechanism for keeping managements on their toes. The more controversial issue concerns whether there is evidence of market failure in the sense that there is excessive and wasteful merger activity in the UK (and in the USA). The argument that fear of takeovers results in harmful 'short-termism' has given rise to a number of suggestions for reforms, but the arguments for and against change are finely balanced.

KEY WORDS

Types of merger	Divorce of ownership from control
Merger boom	
Picking winners	Market for corporate control
De–mergers	Hostile takeover
Management buyouts	Bull market
Corporate raiders	Market correction
Asset–stripping	Short–termism
Contested bid	Non–executive directors
Agreed mergers	Moratorium rule
Institutional shareholders	

Reading list

Foley, P., 'Benefits of the mergers boom', *Lloyds Bank Economic Bulletin*, Sept. 1988.

Harrison, B., *Data Response Questions for A-Level* (no. 11), Oxford University Press, 1986.
Healey, N. and Parker, D., Chapter 2 in *Current Topics in Applied Economics*, Anforme, 1988.
Morison, J. and Shepherdson, I., Chapter 5 in *Economics of the City*, Heinemann Educational, 1991.
Sawyer, M., 'British mergers policy', *Economic Review*, May 1986.
Scouller, J., 'The United Kingdom mergers boom in perspective', *National Westminster Bank Quarterly Review*, May 1987.
Waterson, M., 'Takeovers', *Economic Review*, Nov. 1989.
Wright, M., Thompson, S. and Robbie, K., 'Management buyouts: achievements, limitations and prospects', *National Westminster Bank Quarterly Review*, August 1990.

Essay topics

1. Assess the argument that governments should actively intervene to 'pick winners' and promote changes in the size and organization of industries.
2. 'De-mergers and management buyouts prove that the market sorts out its own mistakes without the need for government intervention.' Discuss.
3. Why do firms merge? Has recent UK experience shown that mergers are in the public interest?
   [Associated Examining Board, 1988]
4. Discuss the factors which should be taken into account in analysing the impact of a proposed merger.
   [Southern Universities Joint Board, 1988]
5. Why has there been an increase in merger activity since 1985? What economic benefits are likely to result from these mergers?
   [Oxford and Cambridge Schools Examination Board, 1987]
6. Assess the extent to which (a) horizontal mergers, and (b) vertical mergers, suppress competition and act against the public interest.
   [University of Oxford Local Examinations Syndicate, 1985]

Data Response Question 3
What is in store?
This task is based on an examination question set by the University of London School Examinations Board in 1989. Read the extract, which is adapted from an article in the *Financial Times* of 26 November 1985, and answer the following questions.

1. Suggest possible reasons why Habitat and Mothercare preferred to merge rather than grow internally.

2. Discuss the likely economic effects of such a merger.
3. Explain how 'the low inflation of the 1980s' exposed the weaknesses of some store groups.
4. Examine the policies, other than those mentioned in the extract, that retail groups may take to increase their share of 'the retail cake'.
5. What does the declining share of consumer spending on retail products tell us about the demand for such products?

The re-shaping of UK retailing in the 1980s found a fresh and surprising impetus with the agreed £1.5 billion merger between the Habitat–Mothercare empire and British Home Stores. Habitat, one of the leading producers of household furniture, had previously acquired Mothercare, one of the main retailers of baby products. British Home Stores was a major chain store supplying clothing and other household products. Such mergers may be only a foretaste of what is to come. Those retailers who have not yet joined the takeover trail have not been idle. Marks and Spencer, for example, is spending almost £500 million over the next two years on a massive programme of store refurbishment and redesign. Why is British retailing being re-vamped in this way?

The moves over the last five years have been prompted by several factors. Firstly, the inefficiencies of retailers in the 1970s were hidden by high inflation. The low inflation of the 1980s has exposed the weaknesses of some store groups. Secondly, retailers have been forced to fight harder for an increasing share of the retail "cake" as consumer spending declined. Thirdly, traditional retailing came under pressure from other types of spending – such as holidays abroad, eating out and private health care. Retail spending fell to about 39 per cent of all consumer spending, down from 43 per cent in 1980 and 53 per cent in 1950.

Chapter Six
Anti-competitive practices

> ... *the predator often has market power and the ability to finance losses for the time necessary to drive out the entrant, often by cross-subsidization from other markets.*

Anti-competitive practices fall into two principal categories – those undertaken by firms together and those undertaken by single firms. Chapter 3 set out the legislative background governing policy on both multi-firm and single-firm practices. Here we consider how the policy has worked in practice and, where appropriate, evaluate possible reforms. The case studies mentioned in the text can be found later in the chapter.

Multi-firm practices

As shown in Chapter 2, agreements by firms to restrict competition, for instance by **price fixing**, are most unlikely to be in the public interest. Consumers suffer through higher prices without there being the prospect of a benefit in the form of possible cost reductions through rationalizing capacity. Thus the UK legislation contains a presumption against **restrictive trade practice** agreements. Those firms which make them must show that they yield identifiable benefits in specified categories. Moreover, all agreements must be notified to the Director General of Fair Trading.

This all sounds very well, but the reality is that many restrictive agreements, often clearly to the detriment of the public, remain in existence for many years because they go unrecorded. Many such agreements are found in the construction industry, where typically major construction projects can only be fulfilled by a relatively small number of firms. Those firms often collude to share the market amongst themselves by fixing tenders. *Case Study A* discusses a particularly flagrant illustration of this in the ready-mix concrete industry.

This suggests strongly that the legislation against price-fixing agreements is not fully effective as many firms can evade the law simply by illegal **non-registration**. Such a practice makes the agreement void in law, but there is no provision in the first instance for criminal proceedings for those involved. Only if a company is proved to have broken court undertakings that it would not conclude restrictive agreements can the company concerned face heavy fines and the directors prison sentences of up to two years for contempt.

What can be done to remedy this unsatisfactory situation? There seems to be a good case for either increasing the penalties for non-registration (and giving the OFT stronger powers of investigation) or for rendering firms concluding them more likely to face law suits from those affected than is now the case.

This second approach would involve the prohibition of, rather than require registration of, restrictive trade practice agreements. It has the advantage of being consistent with European Community legislation on restrictive trade practices (see Chapter 3), and short-circuits the lengthy processes of registration and of the Restrictive Practices Court. The government has indeed put forward proposals of this kind in a White Paper, 'Opening markets: new policy on restrictive trade practices' (July 1989). General prohibition would be combined with special arrangements for the exemption of certain agreements for limited periods either on an individual or block basis and subject to periodic review. It is possible that these legal reforms will be introduced in the next year or two; but until then, enforcement of legislation against price fixing and other arrangements will remain critically weakened.

One important area currently exempt from provisions of the 1976 Retail Trade Practices Act is the **professional rules** imposed upon the legal, medical, dental and related professions. A good example is the rules governing legal services, which in the past have sought to establish mandatory fee scales and bans on advertising. Some of these rules have been investigated by the MMC in the past, and where they restrict or distort competition they have been found to be registrable.

The difficulty in these cases is drawing a distinction between rules which improve the provision of services and those which only benefit the suppliers. Rules designed to maintain standards of competence in a professional practice may fall into the former category, as they do not restrict competition between competent suppliers and may protect the public from charlatans. On the other hand, a blanket prohibition on advertising or the publication of even recommended fee scales may have an adverse effect upon consumers. *Case Study B* looks at the MMC investigation of restrictions on advertising by medical practitioners and illustrates the difficulty in practice of deciding whether rules imposed by a professional body are operating for or against the public interest.

Single firm practices

Single firms may also behave in ways which hamper the working of efficient competitive markets. The analysis of such cases is often more complex, and fine distinctions often have to be drawn between pro-competitive and anti-competitive conduct.

The essential reason for this is that competitive processes inevitably involve rivalries between firms in which they attempt – normally in an impersonal way – to injure another. When one firm cuts the price of its product, it does so in the knowledge that it will take market share from a competitor. The introduction of new products has the same purpose. The observation that one firm's conduct has a detrimental effect on another is not enough to show anti-competitive behaviour. It is normally a sign of the working out of competition.

In this section we consider two main types of potentially anti-competitive behaviour. The first is **predatory pricing** an arrangement whereby a firm cuts its prices for a period in order to drive out a competitor and establish or re-establish a dominant position in the market. The second involves a whole range of practices known collectively as **vertical restraints**; here one firm – normally a manufacturer – imposes restrictions upon another firm – usually a retailer – or on consumers.

Predatory pricing is one of the more dramatic forms of anti-competitive practice. It is likely to occur when a firm enjoying a large market share is threatened by the arrival of an entrant which typically attacks just one of the larger firm's businesses. The large firm reacts by cutting its prices dramatically in the area where the entrant has come in, drives the entrant out of business, and restores prices to their original high level.

Case Studies C and D give two illustrations where such conduct has been found or alleged. The first concerns the bus industry where liberalization of entry in the UK has led to widespread charges of predatory practice. The second is the leading case under European Community law, which at the time of writing is still under appeal.

There are some theoretical grounds for questioning whether it is rational for a firm to behave in a predatory way when threatened by entry. The only way the predator can drive the entrant out of business is by charging low prices for output. Because the predator has the larger market share, the process is likely to be even more costly for it than for the entrant. A predator threatened in only one segment of its business may be able to survive this loss by cross-subsidy; but if it is attacked on several fronts simultaneously or repeatedly in one market, it may not find it profitable to behave predatorily. It might be a better policy to allow the entrant in and share the market. Predation would only be rational if the predator were confident of making higher profits later to compensate for its short-run loss of profit.

Whatever the merits of this argument, whenever predatory pricing has been alleged it has always proved difficult to determine whether the prices are truly predatory. If a firm sells output below its short-run marginal costs, then it is clearly behaving in a predatory way as it is losing money on the deal. But short-run marginal costs may be low in industries where there is surplus capacity. If it were used as a test, then almost no prices would be defined as predatory; so in practice, as the case studies show, other less stringent tests are used. Our own view is that this is a sensible approach, provided it is recognized that it is quite normal and desirable for a firm to cut its prices when exposed to competition.

The second major category of potentially anti-competitive practices performed by a single firm involves vertical restraints; that is, limitations placed by a supplier normally on its retailers. The main practices included in this heading are as follows:

- **Retail price maintenance**: the manufacturer imposes upon the retailer a minimum price at which a product can be sold.
- **Exclusive dealing**: a retailer undertakes to sell only one manufacturer's product, and not the output of rival firms.
- **Territorial exclusivity**: a particular retailer is given sole rights to sell the products of a manufacturer in a specified area.
- **Quantity discounts**: retailers receive progressively larger discounts the more of a given manufacturer's product they sell – this obviously gives them an incentive at the margin to push one manufacturer's products at the expense of another's.
- **Tie-in sales**: restraints which require the retailer to take good X if he or she is to be supplied with good Y – by this means, a manufacturer can extend a monopoly in one market into another, and discourage new entry (by forcing a prospective entrant to come into both markets simultaneously).
- **Long-term supply contracts**: these bind a retailer to a supplier and often can only be terminated by the retailer at great cost.

As with predatory pricing, there is extensive debate amongst economists about the harm involved in these practices. At first sight, many of them seem anti-competitive – in the sense that they either prohibit retailers from discounting products or they prevent other retailers from entering the market. The problem, however, is that almost all of them are capable of economic justification as being potentially to the benefit of consumers, and fashions in economics have fluctuated substantially between condemnation of them and acceptance of them as being in the public interest.

We can illustrate the dilemma by considering the arguments for and against territorial exclusivity. On the one hand, it seems profoundly anti-competitive to allow the manufacturer to license a particular retailer to hold a monopoly of distribution in an area. By restricting the power of other retailers to enter the market, the effect may be to raise prices and damage consumers' interests. On the other hand, territorial exclusivity may operate in consumers' interests in certain cases. Let us take the case of a product which consumers need to examine and test before they buy it. If several retailers are allowed to sell the product in a particular area, each will try to encourage potential buyers to inspect and test the product in other stores and buy it at a discount in their own. Thus no retailer will have an incentive to provide proper inspection or related facilities, but will try to '**free-ride**' on other retailers. As a consequence, consumers in the end will have no facilities to make a proper inspection of the product they intend to buy. With the system of territorial exclusivity, each retailer will have a local monopoly and thus have no opportunity to free-ride on others' facilities. Hence this particular form of vertical restraint may operate in the customers' interest. Similar arguments can be constructed for or against other forms of constraint listed above, although it has proved much harder to produce a convincing argument in favour of retail price maintenance (RPM), which under the Retail Prices Act of 1976 is generally prohibited in the UK.

With the exception of RPM, vertical restraints are for this reason largely taken in the UK on a case by case basis, with emphasis on the effects of a practice rather than on its form. *Case Study E* summarizes the MMC's investigation into a policy adopted by Black and Decker – a **refusal to supply** retailers who sold their drills or workbenches at prices it considered too low.

Case Study A: Price fixing in the ready-mixed concrete industry

Firms entering into restrictive agreements to fix prices or to collude in other ways are obliged to register the agreement with the Office of Fair Trading. The OFT has long suspected that many agreements have gone unregistered. One sector where unregistered cartels have been particularly prevalent is the ready-mixed concrete industry. In the late 1970s, the OFT uncovered a number of cartels operating in this sector and court orders were made against, or undertakings in the courts in place of orders were given by, a number of companies. These companies included Ready Mixed Concrete (Transite) Ltd.

On 17 July 1990, the Director General of Fair Trading announced that he had uncovered eleven covert price-fixing or market-sharing arrangements involving RMC. Because they were not registered, the arrangements were unlawful. Moreover, because RMC and a number of other companies involved were already bound by Orders restricting secret agreements made in the late 1970s the companies were in contempt of court.

In commenting on the agreements, the DGFT noted that he was particularly concerned about the number of construction industry cartels which his office was uncovering. He went on: 'When all the facts are before me I will want to consider taking court action at the earliest opportunity, and this may include action for contempt. . . . I remind those who may have been damaged by the operation of covert cartels by, for instance, being forced to pay higher prices than would otherwise have been necessary, that they have recourse to action through the civil courts where they can sue for damages.' The outcome is described in the accompanying article from the *Financial Times* of 25 September 1990.

Concrete makers face £81,000 contempt fines

SUBSIDIARIES of some of Britain's biggest concrete producers have been fined a total of £81,000 for disobeying court orders prohibiting them from entering unlawful market-sharing and price-fixing agreements.

Two managers, Mr Anthony Hullett of RMC and Mr Peter Hayter, formerly of Smiths, were fined £1200 and £1000 respectively in the first case in which Sir Gordon

Borrie, Director-General of Fair Trading, has taken individuals to the Restrictive Practices Court.

Mr Justice Anthony Lincoln found that four companies, Hartigan Ready Mixed, Pioneer Concrete (UK), Ready Mixed Concrete (Thames Valley) and Smiths Concrete, were guilty of operating price-fixing and market-sharing agreements in 1983 and 1984, contrary to court orders made against the companies and other concrete producers five years earlier. Complaints arose over the supply of ready-mixed concrete in an area around Bicester, Kidlington and Thame in Oxfordshire.

The court was told of 12 meetings in pubs at which the price-fixing and market-sharing deals were worked out, under which it was agreed to split the market with 43 per cent going to Smiths, 21 per cent each to Pioneer and RMC and 15 per cent to Hartigan.

Mr Justice Lincoln said the court was satisfied that the companies and the two managers were guilty of contempt. RMC, Pioneer and Hartigan admitted the contempt charges. Mr Hayter, Mr Hullett and Smiths Concrete denied them.

Ready Mixed Concrete, a subsidiary of RMC Group, the world's biggest concrete producer, was fined £20,000; Smiths Concrete, 49 per cent owned by ARC, the aggregates subsidiary of Hanson, was fined £25,000; Pioneer, part of the Australian group of the same name, was fined £20,000; and Hartigan, 50 per cent owned by Redland, was fined £16,000.

In fixing the fines, Mr Justice Lincoln said the court had taken into account legal costs run up by the parties. RMC had sustained costs of £100,000, Hartigan £75,000 plus £80,000 in respect of a director who was absolved of contempt at earlier proceedings, and Pioneer £300,000. Smiths' costs were also "very heavy".

The court had also taken into account the fact that the unlawful agreements had not affected a nationwide area. The penalties would have been substantially higher had this been the case, the judge said.

The Office of Fair Trading is investigating other allegations of price-fixing in the concrete industry, which it says could lead to further court action.

Andrew Taylor

Case Study B: Advertising and the medical profession

Historically, many professions have imposed restrictions upon the prices their members can charge for services and the extent to which they can advertise their services to members of the public. Throughout the 1970s and 1980s a number of reports by the Monopolies and Mergers Commission and other bodies investigated these restrictions, and the general trend was to strike down price fixing arrangements enforced by professional bodies. The question of advertising proved rather more difficult, with professional bodies expressing concern about advertisements 'knocking' other practitioners, making unsubstantiated claims for the quality of service provided, or forcing practitioners to lower the quality of service to match discounted prices offered by competitors. Despite this, in the second half of the 1980s, a large number of professional bodies relaxed their rules on advertising. These included the Law Society, the Institute of Chartered Accountants, the General Dental Council and the Institute of Structural Engineers.

In 1988, as part of this general trend of questioning restrictions on advertising, the Director General of Fair Trading sent to the Monopolies Commission a reference under the Fair Trading Act 1973 which invited the Commission to consider whether restrictions on advertising imposed on doctors who were either specialists in private practice or general practitioners had the purpose of exploiting or maintaining a monopoly situation and operated against the public interest.

The doctors' professional bodies argued that restrictions on advertising were essential to preserve the relationship of trust between doctor and patient and to protect patients who might be especially vulnerable to promotional advertising. They argued that the unique relationship with the patient meant that comparisons with the advertising rules of other professions were not relevant.

The MMC accepted that relationships between the doctors and their patients often require a higher degree of trust than relationships with other professionals, but at the same time decided that the arguments of the professional bodies were exaggerated. Doctors are already in competition with one another to some degree for patients, and the MMC did not think that overt recognition of the existence of competition need undermine trust and team work between doctors when it is needed.

The MMC therefore concluded that, while restrictions governing advertising to the public by specialist members of the profession did not operate against the public interest, limitations which restrict advertising by specialists to other doctors did operate against it. They also found that restrictions on advertising by general practitioners were against the public interest. The Government welcomed the conclusions and recommendations of the report and asked the DGFT to seek undertakings from the doctors' professional bodies that they would revise their guidance along the lines proposed by the Commission.

Case Study C: Predatory pricing in the bus industry

One of the aims of the Transport Act 1985 was to deregulate local bus services and introduce more competition, thus reducing fares and encouraging new and better services. The Act allowed privately owned bus services to compete with what had formerly been publicly owned monopolies. New entry often had the effect of making the incumbent cut its prices substantially – indeed, this was one of the aims of the Transport Act. But the problem arose that in some cases the incumbent's response may have been designed to drive the entrant out of business and restore the previous monopoly position in which high prices could be charged.

The Office of Fair Trading received a number of complaints from entrants that they were the victim of predatory pricing. Several of these were investigated, and the OFT adopted the practice of considering three factors in the investigation:

(1) whether the structure and characteristics of the market are such as to make predation feasible;
(2) the relationship between revenue and cost;
(3) evidence on the motives and intentions of the firm, including relevant evidence from its behaviour in other markets.

Predation is generally feasible in local bus markets as the predator often has market power and the ability to finance losses for the time necessary to drive out the entrant, often by cross-subsidization from other markets. Once an entrant has been eliminated the predator often has the capacity to raise prices above the competitive level for a long enough period to compensate for any losses incurred while the entrant was being driven out.

In considering the relationship between cost and revenues the OFT takes the view that pricing below short-run variable costs is clearly predatory, but that prices above short-run variable costs can sometimes be predatory. In the case of buses, strictly variable costs comprise wages, fuel and lubricants and tyres. But the OFT regards certain other costs (cleaning, maintenance and vehicle depreciation) as semi-variable. In cases where prices cover strictly variable costs but fall short of variable and semi-variable costs, the OFT considers evidence of motives and intentions.

One case in which the Director General of Fair Trading found predatory pricing to be present involved a local bus service in Inverness. In May 1988, a new company, Inverness Traction Ltd, entered the market previously held as a monopoly by Highland Scottish Omnibuses Ltd. Highland's response to entry was to cut prices considerably and to increase services. The OFT found that the prices charged lay above strictly variable costs, but below the sum of semi-variable and strictly variable costs; it therefore went on to consider evidence of Highland's motives and intentions. It found that some aspects of Highland's behaviour in Inverness suggested predatory intent.

The DGFT referred the matter for investigation to the MMC. The latter's investigation found Highland to have behaved in a predatory way, not only towards the first entrant, Inverness Traction Ltd, but also towards Traction's successor company which was also driven into receivership in November 1989. Thereafter a much larger firm entered the market, and Highland quickly recognized that it could no longer sustain its role as predominant bus operator in Inverness and progressively moderated its competitive response. The MMC thus found that Highland had behaved in a predatory way, but in the light of successful entry by a much larger firm did not consider that remedial action was appropriate. It did note in conclusion that in other circumstances it would be prepared to 'recommend brisk remedial action for anti-competitive action of the sort evinced by Highland'. This decision was, of course, scant consolation for the two victims of successful predatory behaviour.

Case Study D: The European Commission and predatory pricing – the AKZO case

The best known case involving predatory pricing brought before the European Commission concerns AKZO, a large Dutch-based multinational company, and its British subsidiary and a much smaller UK firm called Engineering Chemical Supplies (ECS). Both companies produce organic peroxides which are used as an additive for flour. Before the alleged predatory pricing occurred, AKZO had about 55 per cent of the market for flour additives in the UK and Ireland, with ECS accounting for the bulk of the remainder with a market share of 30 per cent.

Then in 1979 ECS began to sell its products in the plastics sector of the market, offering its products to a longstanding customer of AKZO's at prices which undercut AKZO's by between 15 and 20 per cent. When AKZO responded with price cuts both in the plastics and in the flour additives section of the market, ECS made a complaint to the European Commission under Article 86 of the Treaty of Rome (see Chapter 3).

This case resulted in an out-of-court settlement; but later in December 1982, the Commission decided to conduct its own investigation into the matter and made a dawn raid on AKZO's premises in the UK and the Netherlands. The raid yielded a confidential memorandum outlining decisions made earlier in the dispute which suggested that AKZO contemplated an explicit policy of driving ECS out of business by approaching its customers for flour additives and offering them alternative supplies at very low loss-making prices.

Armed with this documentary evidence, the Commission launched a legal action against AKZO which resulted in the company being fined £6 million for conspiring to engage, and engaging, in predatory pricing. The decision was a controversial one, and is under appeal. Indeed, the Advocate General of the Court of Justice of the European Communities recommended in 1989 that it be overturned. But whatever the outcome of the case, two aspects are especially significant.

Firstly, the Commission's capacity to search premises yielded valuable evidence to assist its prosecution of the case. Secondly, the court's decision implicitly rested on a 'cost-based rule' for determining the presence or absence of predatory pricing. There was nothing wrong in AKZO reducing its prices to its major customers when competition emerged, but the Commission objected to AKZO's efforts to divert the allegiance of ECS's customers by offering them prices which were judged to fall short of average variable costs. The AKZO cases (and the bus cases cited in Case Study C) suggest that both the Commission and the OFT are increasingly relying upon a definition of predatory pricing in terms of the relationship between price and variable costs.

Case Study E: Refusal to supply – the Black and Decker case

One major category of alleged anti-competitive practice involves refusal by a manufacturer to supply certain categories of retailers. The first investigation carried out by the Office of Fair Trading under the Competition Act 1980 involved an investigation of this kind. The issue was whether Raleigh Bicycles was behaving in an anti-competitive way by refusing to supply retailers likely to sell them as 'loss leaders' or which were likely to have no long-term commitment to bicycles. Those refused supply included six national multiple retailers such as Argos, Tesco and Woolworth. Both the OFT and subsequently the Monopolies Commission – to whom the issue was referred – concluded that the company's policy constituted an anti-competitive practice. It is also worthwhile noting that the practice appears not to have benefited the company, whose profits fell substantially.

A similar issue arose more recently in connection with the refusal by Black and Decker to supply domestic power tools and workbenches to certain dealers on grounds that they would be sold at too low a price to the public. Like Raleigh, Black and Decker was concerned that certain retailers with no long-term interest in maintaining the value of the brand would use the products as a loss-leader, the effect of which would be to damage retailers with a longer-term commitment to the product, to reduce the availability of higher-priced products in the firm's range, and to damage the firm's image in the marketplace.

The OFT, and subsequently the MMC, were not impressed by these arguments, and the MMC took the view that it is for the retailer to determine retail selling practices and the retail prices of his goods. In the MMC's view, there was no special public-interest ground to justify the anti-competitive practice. Accordingly the MMC found that the appropriate remedy was for Black and Decker to cease to notify retailers of its required minimum gross margin. The company subsequently gave undertakings to this effect.

Conclusions

We have examined in this chapter a number of instances where suppliers have individually or collectively been suspected of conduct likely to diminish competition. Where several suppliers have been involved, the argument that the practice has operated against consumers' interests has normally been fairly clear-cut. Exceptions arise only in cases where it can be claimed that protection of the public requires the maintenance of minimum standards of competence or of ethical practice. But in some cases these have been a cover for the maintenance of fees at a high level and limitations on advertising services to the public.

Determining the competitive consequences of behaviour by a single firm has proved more problematic. The essential difficulty is that much of the firm's conduct has the intended or unintended consequence of damaging competitors. Some practices, such as normal competition in price and quality, work in consumers' interests. Others may be detrimental to consumers if they are intended to destroy competition or to use a manufacturer's power in relation to its retailers to exclude entry. This chapter has examined a number of leading cases and underlined the difficulty in making a proper determination. If we could clearly identify certain practices as being always or almost always anti-competitive, then it would be possible to adopt a policy of declaring them illegal and rendering any firm practising them liable to civil actions from competitors or customers. Unfortunately, however, there seems no alternative to examining each case on its merits.

KEY WORDS

Price fixing	Exclusive dealing
Restrictive trade practice	Territorial exclusivity
Non-registration	Quantity dicounts
Professional rules	Tie-in sales
Predatory pricing	Long-term supply contracts
Vertical restraints	Free-ride
Retail price maintenance	Refusal to supply

Reading list

Clarke, R., Chapter 11 in *Industrial Economics*, Basil Blackwell, 1985.

Office of Fair Trading, *Anti-Competitive Practices: A Guide to the Provisions of the Competition Act 1990* (available from the Office of Fair Trading).

Essay topics

1. Examine the factors which might give rise to a firm being dominant in a market. Discuss two pricing policies which such a firm might adopt.
   [University of London School Examinations Board, 1989]
2. What factors, in terms of the nature of the product, the number of suppliers and the number of customers, are likely to encourage price-fixing agreements? Discuss the difficulties that might arise in preventing members of a price-fixing arrangement from cheating on their colleagues.
3. Predatory pricing sometimes involves the incumbent firm taking a temporary loss on its output to defeat an entrant. Outline the calculation an incumbent would have to make in deciding whether to follow this policy or to allow the entrant to come in and form a price-fixing arrangement with it.
4. Why does UK legislation adopt an attitude towards resale price maintenance (effectively outlawing it) which is different from that taken towards other vertical restraints such as exclusive dealing?

Data Response Question 4
Plastering the opposition

This task is based on an examination question set by the University of London School Examinations Board in 1988. Read the extract, which is adapted from an article in the *Financial Times* of 21 August 1986, and answer the following questions.

1. Explain what is meant by the following terms as used in the extract: (a) 'discriminated its pricing' and (b) 'exclusive dealings'.
2. What is meant by 'dumping'? Examine the possible reasons why Iberian Trading might dump plasterboard in the UK.
3. Is it necessarily undesirable for BPB Industries to supply 96 per cent of the UK plasterboard market?
4. What are the main factors that determine the price elasticity of demand for plasterboard produced by BPB Industries?

A dispute has broken out in the UK plasterboard industry concerning allegations and counter allegations by BPB Industries, the leading UK manufacturer of plasterboard, and Iberian Trading UK, an importer of Spanish plasterboard.

Iberian Trading UK has convinced the European Commission to begin an investigation into BPB Industries. It was alleged that BPB has abused its dominant position in the UK market in an attempt to eliminate competition in general and Iberian Trading in particular. BPB supplies 96 per cent of the UK plasterboard market.

The allegations included claims that BPB refused to supply, discriminated its pricing against merchants dealing with imported plasterboard, placed restrictions on importers and had exclusive dealings with building merchants. BPB argued that in spite of its dominant position in the UK its plasterboard faces competition from other building materials used for internal partition walls.

BPB Industries countered these claims by making allegations of its own. Two years ago BPB complained to the EEC that Iberian Trading and a Spanish plasterboard manufacturer were dumping plasterboard in the Irish market and were now doing the same in the UK.

Chapter Seven
Regulating monopoly utilities

The beauty of the RPI-X system is that it gives the regulated firm a strong incentive to reduce costs.

In some industries, the ordinary provisions of competition law are considered to be inadequate to control the power of the companies concerned, and special regulations apply. In the UK, these special regulatory regimes apply to industries that have been privatized since 1984 – in particular, telecommunications, gas supply, airports, water and electricity.

The special feature of these industries is that they are often regarded as having at least some elements of **natural monopoly**, discussed in Chapter 4. Remember that a natural monopoly describes an industry where it is most efficient for total demand to be supplied by a single firm, without competition. Figure 12 shows an industry subject to **increasing returns to scale** and hence exhibiting decreasing average cost (AC). If the price were held to P_1 the single firm would just break even and the price of output Q_1 would equal average cost. If, on the other hand, total output of Q_1 were divided equally between two firms each producing Q_2, average costs would

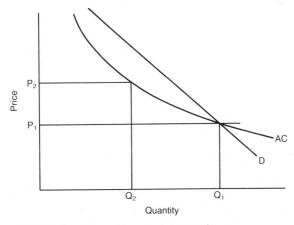

Figure 12 Illustrating increasing returns to scale

rise to P_2, and either the firms would make losses or prices would be forced up.

Many industries that are regarded as natural monopolies have distribution networks which take the service to each household or firm. This clearly applies to telecommunications, gas, electricity and water. In these cases it is quite plausible to argue that allowing two or more companies to set up their own pipes or cables capable of delivering the relevant service in the same area would lead to wasteful duplication and higher costs.

Natural monopolies create particularly difficult problems for the government. In Europe, the tradition until recently has been to take such industries into public ownership and to run them as **nationalized industries**. Because they are publicly owned, the government is able to prevent the company from exercising its monopoly powers to the detriment of consumers. In the USA, by contrast, the policy has for a long time been to allow the companies to be owned by private investors, but to regulate their prices directly. Since 1984, the UK government has led the way in Europe by privatizing many utilities and subjecting them to special regulatory regimes. This has involved the creation of special quasi-independent government agencies to operate these regimes – such as the Office of Telecommunications (OFTEL), the Office of Electricity Regulation (OFFER), the Office of Gas Supply (OFGAS) and the Office of Water Services (OFWAT).

This chapter describes briefly how these special regulatory regimes have operated to protect the public against monopoly and to make the industry behave more 'as if' it were competitive. First, however, it is useful to review whether and how competition can operate in a 'natural monopoly'.

Regulation and competition

When an industry is a natural monopoly, the standard forms of competition often fail to act as a disciplinary device. In particular, entry is not a threat.

The extent of natural monopoly varies from industry to industry. Let us take electricity supply as an example. Three stages are involved in generating electricity and delivering it to domestic and commercial customers. The first stage is the generation of electricity from coal, oil, gas or radioactive materials (nuclear power). The second stage is its transmission at high voltage from the point of generation to a central point within an area of local distribution. In the United Kingdom this is done by the National Grid, which owns and operates the high-voltage cables suspended from pylons or buried in the ground. The third stage is distribution at a much lower voltage to houses or firms.

The *generation* of electricity is not a natural monopoly as power stations can compete with one another over costs. On the other hand, both the National Grid and the local distribution companies are plausibly natural monopolies. An approach to regulating utilities which seeks to maximize competition suggests that the appropriate procedure is to exploit the potential of competition in those parts of the industry that are subject to competitive entry, and to regulate in other ways those that are natural monopolies. Hence the National Grid and local distribution companies will be regulated more closely than generators.

One fairly unsuccessful way of regulating a natural monopoly is to apply what is known in the USA – where it is widely used – as **rate of return regulation**. Under this system, a utility's prices are set by the regulator to allow the firm to earn an acceptable rate of return on its assets. If the firm can show that it is earning a rate of return on its investment which is much less than that earned by other firms or less than it has to pay investors to invest in it, then the regulatory body will allow a price increase to restore profitability.

The problem with this form of regulation is that it provides little or no incentive to the firm to produce efficiently. It is essentially a form of **'cost-plus' pricing**. An efficient firm will be penalized by having its prices held down, as it will show a satisfactory rate of return with low prices, while an inefficient firm will be able to go to the regulatory body, demonstrate a low rate of return and receive a price hike.

Regulatory policy in the UK has attempted to avoid the inefficiencies associated with cost-plus pricing. This has largely involved a method of price-setting described below, known as **price-capping**. But consideration has also been given to developing forms of competition which are consistent with natural monopolies. The aim of these methods of harnessing competitive processes is to substitute for the normal form of competition – competition between firms for customers – some alternative form.

Competitive franchising
Under this system firms compete not *in* the market but *for* the market. That is to say, the right to serve a particular market is allocated by a competitive process, but once the **competitive**

franchise has been granted, competition ceases. An example of this form of competition is the provision in the Broadcasting Act 1990 that the rights to broadcast on ITV or Channel 3 in a particular area of the country should be allocated through a process of competitive tendering (see *Case Study F*). The most efficient firm should be the one willing to pay the most for the right, and the state benefits from the monopoly profits, which are transferred to it from the successful applicant in the form of an annual licence payment. Competitive franchising thus ensures that the industry is supplied monopolistically by the most efficient firm and that the monopoly profits are shifted in the form of licence payments to the government.

Yardstick competition

This is an ingenious system which makes it possible to apply competition across a group of companies each of which has a local monopoly. Let us take the water industry as a potential field for its application. There are ten regional water companies in the UK, as well as many other smaller ones. Suppose that the regulatory body introduced the following scheme for setting water prices: each company would be allowed to charge an amount equal to the average price set by all other companies. The advantage of this scheme is that each company takes the average price as given, and therefore has every incentive to minimize its costs in order to maximize its profits. Thus, provided the companies do not collude, each company individually has an incentive to maintain efficiency. The average for the industry as a whole acts as a **yardstick**, and those firms which are more efficient than average make extra profits while those which are less efficient than average make losses.

It is difficult to introduce yardstick competition explicitly, because of the problem of finding groups of companies sufficiently similar in their circumstances that they can realistically operate to a common average. If geographical or other differences are too great, then it is unfair to set each company's prices as the average of the other companies', as they differ too much for reasons unconnected with their relative efficiency. But regulators find comparative data on efficiency very useful in carrying out their tasks, as *Case Study G*, dealing with the water industry, shows.

Public sector competition

The principle of **public sector competition** is that a part of the industry's assets is kept within public ownership with the aim of keeping the industry 'honest' and prices down to the level of costs. The public sector firm acts as a competitor to the rest of the industry. This approach has not been generally used in the UK because it goes against the principal aim of privatization and may not always lead to efficiency.

Interconnection

Here the natural monopolist continues to own the distribution network, but must make it available to suppliers of competitive services at a regulated price. For example, any company has the right to ship its gas down British Gas' pipelines at rates which are established by OFGAS. Equally, Mercury (BT's rival in the supply of telephone services) has the right to use the BT network at prices which were established by OFTEL. Although there are difficulties in setting charges at levels which both sides recognize as being fair or acceptable, **interconnection** does offer one way of keeping a network in sole ownership but requiring that it be made available to competitors.

The modes of competition described above have had some limited impact upon regulated utilities, but the burden of protecting consumers from monopolistic exploitation still rests largely with more direct forms of price regulation. These are described in the next section.

Price-capping as a means of price control for monopoly utilities

We have seen that one of the major weaknesses of rate-of-return regulation is its lack of an incentive to the firm to increase efficiency. When the first British utility – British Telecom – was privatized in 1984, an attempt was made to overcome this weakness by adopting a different method of price control, known as 'price-capping' or '**RPI minus** x' regulation.

The fundamental logic of price-capping is quite straightforward. The government or regulatory authority sets a limit on the price increases the regulated industry can make over a specified period, normally between five and ten years. Because the restriction applies to the average price increases the firm can make for all its regulated products, it can normally increase the price of some lines above the specified average provided that it keeps the price increase of others below the average. At the time when the price-cap is set, there is uncertainty about the general level of inflation within the economy, so the allowable price increase is set in relation to the general level of inflation as measured by the retail price index (RPI). Thus, after the price-cap for British Telecom was originally set in 1984, the company was allowed to increase the average price of the basket of goods it provides in a regulated context by an amount equal to 3 per cent less than the rate of increase of the RPI. Hence the system was known as 'RPI minus three'. Similar systems have applied to gas, airports, water and electricity, with the value of x in the formula varying in each case. For example, the British Airports Authority is entitled to raise its prices by an amount equal to 1 per cent less than the rate of increase of the retail price index (RPI − 1), with an adjustment for unforeseen costs associated with airport security. Each water company and regional electricity distribution company has a separate value of x determining the extent to which it can raise its prices in relation to the retail price index.

The beauty of the RPI − x system is that it gives the regulated firm a strong incentive to reduce costs. Effectively, the firm faces an increase in its allowable prices which is imposed from outside. If it manages to reduce its costs within the period, its capacity to raise prices is unaffected and it can keep the cost saving as profit. The system is thus free from the fundamental weakness of rate-of-return regulation of natural monopolies − that there is no incentive for the regulated firm to control costs.

There are, however, limitations on the extent to which the mechanism operates. In the first place, an RPI − x regime is normally only specified for a particular period. In the case of British Telecom, that period initially covered the years 1984 to 1989. When the system was reviewed in 1988 the formula was tightened to RPI minus 4.5 per cent for 1989–93.

A second weakness of price-capping is that it gives firms an incentive to reduce the **quality** of the product they sell to consumers. A firm can evade a price-cap by reducing the quality of output: in this respect a reduction in quality is equivalent to a secret price increase. It is therefore essential under a price-capping regime that the regulator monitors the quality of service supplied, even though this involves an investment of energy and resources.

Thirdly, in some cases a regulated utility is unable to control some of the costs to which it is subject. For instance, the price at which the British Gas Corporation can ship gas to households is dependent upon the cost at which it buys gas from suppliers. Any increase or decrease in the latter is more likely to depend upon changes in the world oil market than on the skill with which BGC exercises its business. In such circumstances there is a case for allowing the regulated company to 'pass through' price increases in inputs which are outside its control, and BGC is in fact allowed to do so.

Case Study F: Competitive franchising in broadcasting

The right to operate a television franchise in the UK has been an extremely valuable one. In the 1950s the government set up the ITV system as a group of regional monopolies for television which is financed by advertising. Because television is a very powerful advertising medium, the companies have been able to earn considerable revenues, especially in the larger ITV regions such as London, Central and TVS (the south). In the 1960s one broadcaster famously referred to an ITV franchise as 'a licence to print money'.

ITV and other broadcast licences have hitherto been distributed through a quasi-competitive process in which applicants seeking to hold a licence lasting 10 or 15 years applied to the Independent Broadcasting Authority (IBA) for the licence. The IBA would then assign the licence to what it considered to be the best applicant, using a range of criteria including programming plans, personnel, financial strength and the regional links. This system has come in for serious criticism because of the perceived arbitrariness of many of the judgements.

The Broadcasting Act of 1990 introduced a more transparent form of competition for licences based upon the applicant's willingness to pay. The procedure for assigning licences for the present ITV system covering the period 1993 to 2002 is to be as follows. Applicants submit to the new regulatory body (the Independent Television Commission) information about their programme plans and their financial prospects, and a cash bid for the licence, payable in annual instalments. Any applicant who fails to pass the so-called quality hurdle – a threshold level of programme provision and financial solvency established to weed out unsuitable applicants – is eliminated. Those who survive this test then have their cash bids examined, and the licence is awarded (except in carefully defined exceptional circumstances) to the company offering the most.

The procedure is thus intended to combine competition for a licence with the recognition that only a limited number of regional licences are available. The quality hurdle ensures that broadcasters will provide an adequate level of service, while the bidding process means that the state gets the benefit of any monopoly profits, and that the licence goes to the most efficient firm. The proposals in the Act have proved controversial, especially among holders of current licences who may be displaced by higher bidders. It remains to be seen how the system will work out in practice, but it is a good example of competitive franchising.

Case Study G: Yardstick competition in the water industry

When the water industry was privatized in 1989, it took the form of 10 large regional water authorities and 29 smaller statutory water companies. Soon after the privatization, a proposal came forward to merge three of the smaller water companies under the control of a large French company, Compagnie Generale des Eaux. In accordance with the Water Act, the proposed merger was referred to the Monopolies and Mergers Commission.

The water industry has many characteristics of a natural monopoly, as it is clearly inefficient for two sets of water and sewerage pipes to service the same street. At the same time the industry does provide possible scope for yardstick competition, as a substantial number of water companies are operating side by side. The regulatory body for water, OFWAT, thus has the potential to compare costs across companies and form views about their relative efficiency. These views can then be fed into the price capping process: a company found to be inefficient would receive a higher target for cost reduction than one found to be efficient.

In evidence to the MMC, the Director General of Water Services (DGWS) argued that, under Section 30 of the Water Act, those proposing the merger of independently controlled water companies had to accept a burden of proof that there were substantial gains in terms of cost reductions which could be passed on to consumers and which could not be achieved in other ways; and moreover that these outweighed the effects on OFWAT's ability to encourage efficiency by comparing the performance of water enterprises. The DGWS said that he was worried that the number of independently controlled water companies was significantly lower than 30, and suggested that any further reduction through merger would have to yield substantial gains in cost reduction to consumers.

The MMC recommended that the merger should be allowed to go ahead on condition that all the cost savings from the merger are passed on to consumers; that no class of water user should pay more than would have been the case had the merger not taken place, in each of the first 10 years after the merger; and that each of the three water companies is run as a separate profit centre, providing the DGWS on request with comparative data.

In the event the Trade Secretary tightened the conditions, and only approved the merger following a promise by the three companies to pass savings equal to 10 per cent of costs on to customers. This conclusion shows that even though yardstick competition is not a formal element of the price-capping process, cost comparisons are implicitly valued at a high rate by the regulatory system.

Conclusions

Certain vital **network industries** provide particularly difficult problems for competition policy. Because some parts of them are natural monopolies, some services can most efficiently be supplied by a single firm. Strong measures are thus necessary to prevent monopolistic exploitation of consumers, often involving some form of detailed price control.

It is vital that such price controls should as far as possible give the firm in question an incentive to reduce costs. The US model of regulation of utilities lacks such incentives because it is at bottom a cost-plus system: the firm is allowed to recover its costs and to earn a small profit in addition. In the UK a different form of regulation – price-capping – has been introduced. Within the period for which the price-cap is fixed, the firm has a clear incentive to behave in an efficient way and minimize costs. But if the price-cap is adjusted too frequently in accordance with observed levels of profitability, this desirable incentive property may disappear. It is also necessary to supplement the price-cap with direct controls on the quality of output to prevent deliberate quality degradation.

The tendency at present in the UK is to stick with RPI minus x regulation while at the same time making every effort possible to expand the area of competition – and hence reduce the need for regulation. Thus, the major review of telecommunications policy undertaken in 1990 resulted in proposals for greater freedom of entry into the industry; if successful, these policies might ultimately lead to a lower level of regulation.

KEY WORDS	
Natural monopoly	Yardstick
Increasing returns to scale	Public sector competition
Nationalized industries	Interconnection
Rate of return regulation	RPI minus x
Cost-plus pricing	Quality
Price-capping	Network industries
Competitive franchise	

Reading list

Davies, G. and Davies, J., 'The revolution in monopoly theory', *Lloyds Bank Review*, July 1984.

Helm, D., 'Regulating privatized industries', *Economic Review*, March 1990.

Hurl, B., Chapters 4, 5 and 6 in *Privatization and the Public Sector*, Heinemann Educational, 1988.

Robinson, C., 'Economics of electricity privatization', *Economics: Journal of the Economics Association*, autumn 1989.

Essay topics

1. 'Monopoly is against the public interest. Nationalized industries are monopolies. Nationalized industries should therefore be abolished.' Discuss.
   [University of Cambridge Delegacy of Local Examinations, 1988]
2. Explain what is meant by market failure. Discuss whether or not monopoly in the supply of electricity is sufficient to justify the industry's continued public ownership.
   [Joint Matriculation Board, 1989]
3. How might the pricing and output decisions of a monopoly be affected by whether it operated within the public or private sector of the economy?
   [Southern Universities Joint Board, 1989]
4. Does the record of privatized companies support the case for further privatization?
   [Oxford and Cambridge Schools Examination Board, 1990]

Data Response Question 5

Gas pressure

The following is adapted from a Press Release of OFGAS dated 11 June 1990. Read the piece and then answer the following questions.

1. Explain why 'gold plating' of service is a danger if a company is subject to rate-of-return regulation.
2. Explain why a company subject to a price-cap might be tempted to lower its standard of service below acceptable levels.
3. The price-cap applying to British Gas only affects its small – chiefly domestic – customers. Why is it considered unnecessary to cap the prices British Gas charges to its industrial customers?
4. Discuss the difficulties OFGAS would have in estimating the sort of cost savings which British Gas should be able to make in running its business.

Regulator to review gas price formula

The gas industry's regulator, Mr James McKinnon, today announced the setting up of a review of the price formula which controls the price of gas to Britain's 17 million domestic users.

He said, 'People using up to 25,000 therms of gas each year must be assured that the formula governing the price they pay gives them a fair deal. It is essential, therefore, that OFGAS achieves its twin goals of: ensuring tariff customers get the best possible value for money; and allowing British Gas to run its business as efficiently as possible.'

Mr McKinnon added: 'The relationship between British Gas and its regulator is now at the crossroads and the outcome of the review will determine the direction for Britain's gas supply industry in the next decade. The review will assess whether the British Gas service commitment constitutes value for money and whether domestic prices are properly related to the standard of service offered. There should be no "gold plating" of service, if unnecessary costs are required to provide that service, and British Gas should not increase its profitability by lowering its standards of service below acceptable levels.'

He said the review would address a number of major issues arising from the structure of the formula, including:

- whether or not British Gas is getting a fair profit in the domestic market in relation to the degree of risk involved;
- the sort of cost savings British Gas should be able to make in running its business.

Index

Asset stripping 54

Big Bang (Stock Exchange) 32
Bull market 59
Burden of proof 31

Cartel 34, 35, 70
Collusion 12
Competition
   perfect 4, 5
   workable 8
Competitive franchising 81
Consumer surplus 6, 7
Contested bid 55
Corporate raiders 54
Cost-plus pricing 81, 88

Dawn raid 13
Demergers 53, 54, 63
Divorce of ownership from control 59
Dominant position 18

Economies of scale 55, 56
Entry barriers 36 – 42
   innocent 39, 40, 48
   legal 38, 39
   strategic 41, 42, 48
European Commission 18
European Court of Justice 19
Exclusive dealing 68

Franchise, television 85, 86
'Free-rider' 69

Gateways 31
Greenmail 15
Guinness plc 3, 61

Hostile takeover 57

Industrial Reorganization Corporation 53
Information agreements 31
Insider dealing 60
Institutional shareholders 56
Interconnection 83

Junk bonds 14

Leveraged buyout 14
Long-term supply contracts 68
Loss-leader 76

Management buyout 13, 54, 63
Market for corporate control 12, 56
Markets, contestable 8, 27
Mergers
   boom 52
   conglomerate 51, 52
   control regulation 21, 60
   horizontal 50, 51, 63
   vertical 51, 63
Monopoly 5
   complex 36, 37, 41, 44, 45, 46
   natural 39, 40, 79, 81
   simple 36, 44
Moratorium rule 61

Nationalized industries 80
Network industries 88

OFWAT 86, 87
'One-stop shopping' 21